T0078191

When an Ordinary Man has a Supernatural Encounter with an Extraordinary Spirit, life is

Transformed!

Second Edition

DAVID CARPENTER

authorHOUSE®

AuthorHouse™ UK Ltd.
500 Avebury Boulevard
Central Milton Keynes, MK9 2BE
www.authorhouse.co.uk
Phone: 08001974150

First Edition published by AuthorHouse 20/8/2007
This Second Edition, with additional Chapter, published by AuthorHouse 13/5/2013

ISBN: 978-1-4817-9250-9 (sc)
ISBN: 978-1-4817-9251-6 (e)

This book is printed on acid-free paper.

Because of the dynamic nature of the Internet, any web addresses or links contained
in this book may have changed since publication and may no longer be valid.

The views expressed in this work are solely those of the author and do not necessarily reflect
the views of the publisher, and the publisher hereby disclaims any responsibility for them.

Table of Contents

Introduction

This is a book about a very ordinary man in an ordinary job with an unremarkable, even bog-standard lifestyle. He's not especially talented, or virtuous, and he definitely has faults and limitations, at least as many as most. This is the true story about what happens after that ordinary man has a supernatural encounter with an extraordinary spirit. That encounter happened in moments. The effect reverberated through the years, causing a complete transformation of every aspect of life and self.

This book has been some years in the writing. It began as a brief account to answer the questions of clients curious about the journey from young salesman, via social worker and probation officer, to hypnotherapist, counsellor and psychotherapist. As clients asked questions not answered by what was already written, the book grew piece by piece as more and more was added.

The idea of turning it into a book for publication grew out of a suggestion made by a client who read an early version of it. I had never considered such an idea, but to this client, a successful published author, it was an obvious logical progression, and she expressed some surprise that I had not considered publication already.

There are many others whose contributions have made the book and its subject matter possible. Wise mentors have appeared along the journey, exactly when needed, and their contributions are detailed in the book. These include Jack Hardwick, pastor of the Pinhoe Fellowship in Exeter, Tom Marriott, at that time the leader of Church House Trust in Essex, Malcolm Worsley, Director of Linkup in Nuneaton when first we met, and Guy Cornwall-Jones, who was Rector of St James' Church in Weddington.

Many others have stepped into my life to provide small but essential pieces of help, exactly when required, and I am grateful to each for their influence. In addition, I should acknowledge the immense amount of learning and experience I owe to many who have been colleagues, and to those who have been clients during the years as social worker, probation officer, hypnotherapist, counsellor and psychotherapist. These latter must remain anonymous here, for reasons of confidentiality. Finally, I must pay tribute to my wife Maggie, the wisest woman I have ever met, whose support, encouragement, commitment and love since our marriage in 1972 I consider to be one of the greatest of the many blessings in my life.

Chapter I

The Journey Begins

"You'd better start praying," he said, staring straight at me. His soft Irish voice somehow made his words even more frightening. "Because I'm going to count to three, then I'm going to stab you." I felt very frightened; I really didn't know what to do, and I guess that showed. "You can pick up a knife from the table there if you want to and defend yourself", he said. I knew that would be useless; this man was far more used to violence than I was. The chain of events that led to this moment began many months before.

As I drove to work at the start of that ordinary day, I had no idea that the events of that day were going to change my life dramatically and permanently. In my early twenties, I was fairly 'successful'. I had been a management trainee with a major motor manufacturer, and then worked in the marketing division of that same company. Now I was working in sales for a pharmaceutical company, visiting medical practitioners in general practice and in hospitals, discussing the company's medicines and their use. That meant a very good salary, and a new company car every year. I was married to a beautiful wife, Maggie, and we had a nice three-bedroom semi detached house in Chelmsford, just outside London. There was another side to all this. Work was completely unfulfilling; my marriage was going badly; I was drinking more than was good for me; I had begun using amphetamines ("speed") to get the energy and motivation to go to work each day. Still, the 'success symbols' I had accumulated made it easy for me to blind myself to all this, and to tell myself that I was doing well.

On this particular day, I was trying to be a bit too clever. I was late for an appointment with a consultant surgeon at a hospital, so I was taking a short cut through back streets to avoid traffic, and driving at speed: along roads with a 30 mph speed limit, I guess I was driving at around 50 miles an hour. I didn't even notice the crossroads at which I should have given way, or the lorry that had right of way, until a split second before the lorry hit the offside rear wing of my shiny new company car. I swerved over the crossroads, out of control.

The collision knocked me sideways, knocking my glasses off, and as I tried to sit upright and stamp on the brake pedal, I hit the accelerator in stead. The car careered out of control, headlong into a parked car, travelling at about 50 mph. I had no seat belt on. By 'coincidence' (the first of many I was to experience) the owner of the car had forgotten – for the first time ever, she later assured me – to apply the handbrake. So instead of me flying forward face first through the windscreen, much of the momentum was absorbed by the other car – which sped off down the road, mounted the curb, smashing a fence before coming to a stop in a front garden.

Someone called the police. (That was entirely appropriate, as I had been driving very badly.) As I stood waiting for them in the street, something about the accident brought me face to face with the fact that my life so far was a mess, and that nothing I had done so far was worth the quarter of a lifetime or so I had taken over it. There came to mind a book I had read when I was about 15 years old – The Cross and the Switchblade, by David Wilkerson. He had been a minister in a little church in the USA when suddenly, at a time when he was praying, he felt that God was calling him to work in the 'ganglands' of New York, among the pimps, prostitutes, heroin addicts, drug dealers and gang members. The book was an account of the amazing ways in which he was guided – either by God, or by million-to-one coincidences – to establish a project to reach out to those people.

An example came to mind. Many gang members and others were touched by his preaching, had turned their backs on their old ways and become Christians. He had established a hostel for them, so that they could get away from their old associates as part of their rehabilitation. The hostel had no regular source of funds – it was financed by faith. One day, there was no money left in the bank account, and no food in the larder. Dave Wilkerson assembled the residents of the hostel in the room that was set aside as a chapel. He told them that God had promised to supply their needs, and that they should pray.

After they had been praying for some time, a woman walked into the chapel. She had been knocking at the door for some time, but had not been heard. As the door was open, she had walked in. At the very time they had begun praying in the hostel, she'd had a sudden impulse to do something completely out of character for her – to empty her piggy bank and to bring the money to him. The money was enough to provide all they needed.

As I stood in the road next to the crashed car, I felt more and more urgently the desire for the purposeful, guided, worthwhile life that Dave Wilkerson had. I prayed for the first time in years, something like:

> "Lord, I'm useless at managing my life and what I'm offering you is worthless – but please take it anyway. Come into my life now. Take me, take my life, and just use me to do something worthwhile."

Almost immediately, I felt the touch of someone far more powerful than I, and a certainty that I was not meant to be the 'dynamic young sales executive' with the flash suits and the company car; I was meant to be giving God's love to those who needed it. I phoned my mother, and she drove to collect me by car (my car was badly damaged and undriveable) and when I walked back into our home, my wife Maggie looked at me with some concern, asking me if I was all right. I remember my reply as I shook my head in puzzlement: "I don't know – I think I want to be a vicar!"

A few weeks later, it was Easter Bank Holiday Monday. Maggie and I had begun praying together now and then. When we prayed together on that day, I remember feeling very certain that we should go to Cambridge. We remembered hearing that there was a project there run by the Cyrenians, a community house for 'single homeless men' (dosser alcoholics, junkies, etc.). We had no idea where the project was, so when we had driven to Cambridge, we asked at the police station, and they gave us directions. Even so, we walked past the place three times before we realised that derelict building must be the place.

It was a derelict pub, condemned years before as unfit to live in, and all the windows we could see were boarded up. The front door was a sheet of chipboard, like that covering the windows, but there was a push button next to it, and when I pushed it, we could just hear the sound of a bell ringing, somewhere in the building. The heavy front door opened a crack, with a heavy iron chain preventing it from being opened further. Two eyes and a beard peered at us through the tiny opening. When we explained what we wanted the door was opened, and we were welcomed into an amazing place. Inside were the residents, mostly dosser alcoholics, plus a few junkies, ex-mental hospital patients, and others, and the workers, young people like us, mostly students at the university there. The filthy old carpets were threadbare on the floorboards, the plaster was literally falling off the walls. The windows that didn't face the street were not boarded up: in place of glass they had polythene sheets pinned with drawing pins across the wooden frames. A faint aroma of unwashed bodies seemed all-pervasive. The place was a terrible fire risk, and the workers took it in turns to do 'night duty', sitting up all night, staying awake in case of fire.

Something happened to me as we walked into that place and met the people there. If you've ever had toothache you will know how soon you begin ignoring that background pain, almost to the point of being unaware of it. You will also know the wonderful feeling of the absence of pain after the dentist has dealt with it. All my life there had been a background pain, and because it was always there, I had never realised it. It was the pain of not really belonging, or not being in the place where I was meant to be.

As I walked into that dilapidated building, the pain disappeared. For the first time in my life, I experienced the feeling of being in exactly the place I was meant to be. I knew that this was the place we would be coming to. Maggie, independently of me, had a similar sense of certainty, though in her case combined with a certain trepidation! Some weeks later, we were interviewed by the committee of local people who administered the charity that ran the project, and they were very happy to invite us to become full time volunteers, working in the project.

Before we could begin working at the Cyrenians, we needed to sell our house: once we were full time volunteers, we would have no way to pay the mortgage. (Cyrene volunteers received their board and lodging, plus an amount of pocket money exactly equal to the amount of money that remained to a resident in receipt of benefit, after paying his rent.) We placed the house with a number of estate agents, but many weeks later there had been absolutely no interest at all. (This was a time of recession for the housing market, and houses were simply not selling.) Accustomed to being self reliant, I put a huge advert in the local paper – this was 1974, and the ad cost £35 – a very large sum at that time.

Weeks later, that expensive ad had done nothing to help. I was wondering what on earth I should do next. It was 11.30 at night, and Maggie had gone to bed. I found myself thinking and wondering: maybe I should pray for a buyer...?

It may seem strange to you, the reader, that I had not done this before. As a child, I had gone to Sunday school at a Church of England church, and earned extra pocket money by singing in the choir. After my recent conversion, I had begun attending the local Church of England church, but do not remember anyone there speaking or teaching about the idea that God works **today** in the lives of ordinary people, and certainly I remember no teaching about the real effectiveness of prayer – maybe I wasn't listening hard enough.

Anyway, I decided that it wouldn't do any harm to pray about the problem: after all, I'd tried everything else I could think of. So, a little before midnight, I knelt down on the floor, resting my arms on the sofa, and began to pray. It was not a very elegant prayer: I was feeling pretty frustrated and angry, and more than a little uncertain too: as you know, it's hard to give up an established career. However, more by good fortune than good judgement, what I said and my state of mind precisely fulfilled the criteria for really effective prayer. It went something like this:

> **"Lord, I'm <u>SURE</u> that you're calling us to work at the Cyrenians! So you <u>MUST</u> want us to sell the house, because we couldn't possibly pay the mortgage! So if you want us to go to the Cyrenians, then <u>*SEND A BUYER!!!*</u>**

I had been on my knees for around a minute when, to my irritation and annoyance, the telephone started ringing. ("Who on earth is inconsiderate enough to disturb us this late at night?") I answered the phone, and a voice said, "I'm sorry to disturb you this late at night, but I've been looking at an old copy of the Essex Chronicle, and there's an advert for your house in it – is it still for sale by any chance?"

That's the person who bought our house. And that was one of many answers to prayer that have become a normal part of our lives since then. The prayer was effective because it was asking for what was needed to fulfil what God was calling us to do. (**If** you are calling us to do this **then** give us what we need to do what you have told us to do...)

Chapter 2

Cambridge Cyrenians

The Cyrenians was an umbrella organisation, to which individual projects for single homeless could affiliate. The national central organisation provided a number of services to the individual projects, including a central clearinghouse for many prospective volunteers who contacted the central organisation, and other kinds of support, including providing some training conferences for volunteers. Later, at one of those conferences, we met some of those in salaried work for National Cyrenians. They were every bit as idealistic as us volunteers, genuine people who were doing the work with a sense of mission.

The Cyrene house at East Road, Cambridge was, unbeknown to us, a place with a reputation, within the wider Cyrenian organisation, for being a place of constant drama and crisis. It was a 'short term house', which meant that those living as residents there were expected to make moves, within a few months of arriving, to leave again, preferably to return to more normal living. Its reputation as a place of drama and crisis was well deserved. When we arrived, there were around a dozen residents, mostly dosser alcoholics, and each one was a unique character. These men often came and went very quickly, and there are certainly many that I cannot recall. Some of those we knew, however, come readily to mind.

There was Johnny, an amiable if somewhat eccentric Scotsman. He always claimed that his brother was a certain famous union leader often seen on television. He had the same surname, so that may well have been true. He was there when we arrived, and for the first week or two we privately wondered why on earth he was there: he seemed such a competent man, friendly and capable. Then he had the first of the drinking bouts, which, we were to discover, were a regular punctuation to his life. For many days he was constantly unsteady on his feet; his speech was slurred; his breath smelt constantly of 'jack'. This unsavory drink was the normal tipple of the dosser-alcoholic community there, though I have found it nowhere else. The recipe was simply. Buy a quart bottle of cider from the off-licence, and a small bottle of surgical spirit from the chemist. Drink a few inches off the top of the cider, and add the surgical spirit. Mix well, and drink slowly.

The rule of the house, as with all Cyrene houses throughout the country, was that no alcohol was allowed anywhere in the house, so Johnny would go out somewhere to drink, and then return. This would continue for some days. He would then miraculously sober up, and for many weeks he was again the gentle humorous man who had originally made us wonder why he was there.

There was Pete. He had served in the armed forces in better times. Although we workers were far younger than he (I guess he was close to 60 years old) he would invariably stand to attention if we spoke to him, and would always address me as 'sir'. Because of my youth, this felt a little strange, I remember…

Then there was Matt. Another Scotsman. I seem to remember him telling me that he had been a fisherman. Unlike many of the other men there, I don't think I ever detected the smell of 'jack' on his breath, though he was certainly drunk from time to time.

A star of the place was a man I only ever knew as 'Punch', a short, stocky, grey haired Irishman who I guess was in his very late 50s or early 60s. He was already well established in the house when we arrived. The story was that he had been found by a Cyrene worker, sleeping rough and obviously very ill – close to death, apparently. He had been taken into the house and nursed back to health. His voice was always very loud – not shouting, just much louder than anyone else's, as though the volume knob had stuck.

Big Jon was another character. He was very overweight, but seemed to be able to get about in spite of this. He was almost blind – a fact that he kept from the other men because he was afraid (with some justification) that he would be bullied or taken advantage of if they knew how little vision he had left. Someone told us that the blindness was the result of years of drinking methylated spirits – that is to say, pure alcohol to which has been added a little methyl alcohol to render it poisonous, and thus (theoretically) undrinkable. Years later I was to find out that blindness is indeed the first symptom of methyl alcohol poisoning, followed by insanity, then death. Looking back at his occasionally eccentric behaviour, I wonder whether the deterioration in his sanity had already begun.

These were a few among the dosser alcoholics who made up the majority of the residents. One or two of the resident group were different. Martin, for example, was not an alcoholic but a heroin addict. He was in his early twenties, and around my height. He was, however, a fraction of my weight and painfully thin, with skin as near to white in colour as I have ever seen. He was a pitiful soul, apparently determined to please all of the people all of the time. His arms had angry sores as a result of repeatedly injecting heroin. He was now a registered drug addict, and went to the chemist each day to get his prescription for his daily dose of the heroin substitute methadone. However, from time to time he would supplement this with injections of illicit heroin, which he often seemed able to acquire – how he paid for this is a mystery.

I remember a fellow worker at the hostel telling me that Martin had confided to him that he had great difficulty finding a blood vessel in his arms or legs to inject into, because these had deteriorated through repeated drug use, and that in his desperate search for a vein into which to inject, he had begun to inject into veins in his penis. I am sure that my fellow worker was reporting accurately what Martin had told him, though I have no way of knowing whether Martin was telling the truth. We workers had been told that under no circumstances were we to try to persuade Martin to cease his use of the drugs, because the doctors considered that he was now too weak to be able to tolerate the withdrawal symptoms.

I remember another young man, a big, gentle and deferential soul, who had been a cook in the catering corps in the army until he had been diagnosed as schizophrenic. He had been discharged from the army, the reason given being, 'services no longer required'. He carried around with him a battered photograph of himself in army uniform, of which he seemed inordinately proud. He was staying at the house because, having been discharged from psychiatric hospital, he simply had nowhere else to go.

It was inevitable, with so many people, and so many different kinds of people, living together, that interpersonal problems and difficulties would arise from time to time. A feature of the project was the regular meetings to discuss and resolve difficulties. First, there were regular house meetings. Attendance at these was theoretically compulsory for all, though a resident's absence was sometimes overlooked. These would often be discussing matters as small as whether or not everyone was doing their fair share of the washing up. Trivial as that may sound, I have seen residents – grown men – ready to come to blows about whether someone is avoiding his fair share of the chores.

Then, for workers, there were the Brother Keith meetings. Brother Keith was an Anglican Franciscan Friar, part of the Franciscan community doing social work in Cambridge. In many places, the sight of Brother Keith, in his brown Franciscan habit, with sandals on his bare feet, walking through the streets, at the very least would have turned heads. In Cambridge, people hardly noticed. He was also a remarkably strong, gentle and spiritual man – exactly the right person to get a group of workers talking about what was on their mind. This was, at the time, quite difficult for me. I had been used to keeping my thoughts to myself, and the idea of really getting everything into the open and talking things through fully was new and more than a little threatening. Attending Brother Keith meetings was one of the many ways in which I was learning important lessons that were to stand me in good stead later.

Cyrene projects had a four-fold rule by which they were managed: no alcohol or drugs on the premises, no violence on the premises, attendance at house meetings, and regular payment of rent (paid by Social Security rent voucher by those claiming benefits.) While failure to attend house meetings was often tolerated or overlooked in practice, breaking of any of the other three rules meant instant eviction from the house. Living in Cambridge at that time was another group of dosser alcoholics, all of whom were banned from the house for violation of those rules – usually for violations of the rule about violence. We workers called them 'the heavy gang'. At irregular intervals, members of the heavy gang would come to the door, which we would open on a chain. They would ask for a sandwich, or a cup of tea, or other favours. We would usually give them what they asked for, in part because we knew they had few other sources of sustenance, apart from what they were able to beg from passers by in the streets and the seriously inadequate daily benefit paid by Social Security to those of no fixed abode.

Their lifestyle was a simple one. Wake up under the bridge where they had spent the night. Have a wash and a drink of water at a public lavatory, then start walking the streets, begging from passers by. (I understand that this was sometimes a very lucrative, if unreliable source of income, with a combination of university students and tourists ensuring good pickings at times.) Then off to the nearest off licence and to the chemist to buy the ingredients for 'jack'. Later in the day, if the fruits of begging had been sparse, call at the Cyrene house to beg a sandwich, then finally back to your spot under the bridge at the end of the day, making sure that you have enough 'jack' left to ensure that you will sleep (or pass out) despite the uncomfortable conditions. Relationships between Cyrene workers and the heavy gang were usually pretty amiable – they knew that they were not allowed in, and usually (though not always) accepted that. One or two of the heavy gang are worth mention here.

Big Jim was undoubtedly the leader of the group, inasmuch as there was any leader. A huge man, probably closer to seven feet tall than to six, he had obviously once been a fine figure of a man. Now the combination of alcohol abuse, methyl alcohol poisoning, sleeping rough and advancing years had taken their toll, weakening this giant considerably. During severe weather in past winters, he had been allowed into the Cyrene house, suffering from pneumonia. Unfortunately, whenever he returned to any semblance of health, he would become violent again, so once he was over the worst of his illness, he would revert to his previous 'banned' status. I think that he was actually happier living under the bridge, as long as his health allowed.

Another memorable member of the heavy gang was never known by any other name than 'the Dog Man'. A jack drinker like most of the others, he was usually accompanied by a greyhound, and man and dog were obviously devoted to each other. I understand that when the proceeds of begging were sparse, buying food for the greyhound took precedence over food for the owner. The dog man and his canine companion had a unique way to earn money. The dog man would sell the handsome looking dog to someone (usually a tourist) who expressed an interest. We all knew when this had happened, as the dog man would be seen for days on end, minus dog and drunk as a lord. Then the money would run out, and he would go into a deep melancholy, worrying that he had lost for good the dog who was his closest friend. However, the dog always managed to escape from his new owners, however far away he had been taken, and would invariably return to his master. Usually, a week or so after being sold, the animal was back, looking sleek and well fed, and all was well again in the dog man's world.

The other really memorable member of the heavy gang was Mickey. He was a comparatively young looking Irish man, and we had been warned to take care if he was around, as he had already served several terms of imprisonment for wounding and other serious violent offences. He would come to the door, like the others, begging for food. We would usually give him a sandwich, but took even more care than usual to keep the chain on the door! He was one of the very few that seemed to me to be a really scary person to have around. Even when he was being amiable and trying to curry favour, there was always a sense of the threat of violence in the background.

Incidents of high drama were virtually a daily occurrence in the project. I soon lost count of the number of times I stood between men who were about to fight. If I had tried to physically prevent them, I would undoubtedly have been severely injured, as even the most unfit among them was far more experienced in violent conflict than I. So I soon developed another way of dealing with such situations. I would tell the prospective combatants, as I stood between them, that I was certainly not going to use violence, but that if they wanted to injure each other, they would have to injure me first, as I was going to continue to stand between them. This gentle and outwardly confident approach to violence was always successful – in part, I believe, because I was genuinely prepared to be injured or worse, if God chose to allow that to happen, and sure that God had the power to protect me from such results if He did not intend it.

One example of this stands out in my memory. Residents were, of course, free to come and go as they pleased. Most, however, would ask a worker to let them out when they were leaving the house. This was because a member of the heavy gang might well be nearby, and residents were too frightened to refuse them admission to the house if they demanded it. On a number of occasions, we found one or another of the heavy gang in the house, having somehow gained admission. We would then have to 'talk them out', as we called it, or in other words persuade them to leave. This often took some time, especially if it was raining outside, but it was an important task, because the atmosphere of fear in the house would be immediate and very strong, as the word swiftly went round the resident group that a member of the heavy gang was in the house.

On this occasion, a resident had asked me to let him out. It was evening, and dark outside. I seem to remember it was raining. I opened the front door and he left. As I was about to close the front door, suddenly Mickey, the heavy gang member, was standing in the doorway. He demanded to be let into the house. I mildly reminded him that he was banned, and that meant that I was not allowed to let him in. Behind me in the entrance hall was a table, on which someone had left some cutlery. I was wearing a wooden cross on a leather thong around my neck. He gestured to the cross contemptuously with his head. "What's that around your neck?" he asked. I quietly told him what he already knew, that it represented what I believed in.

"You'd better start praying," he said, staring straight at me. His soft Irish voice somehow made his words even more frightening. "Because I'm going to count to three, then I'm going to stab you."

I felt very frightened; I really didn't know what to do, and I guess that showed.

"You can pick up a knife from the table there if you want to and defend yourself", he said. I knew that would be useless; this man was far more used to violence than I was. I heard his voice beginning the count. "ONE!..." Suddenly, I knew what I had to do. I prayed silently for a moment. Then I turned my back on the man, and began to walk away from him, **_very slowly_**.

"TWO!..." I heard the voice behind me, and I remember silently telling God that I was His, and that I was prepared to be stabbed if He chose to allow it. I had heard that when one is stabbed, it doesn't feel sharp, more like a punch, and that people often do not realise they have been stabbed till they see their own blood. I wondered how it would feel. I walked very slowly, waiting for the count of three. In stead, I heard Mickey's voice saying, "Huh! I suppose you're going to call the police now!" I slowly turned around to face the door. The open door was moving slightly in the breeze. The light of the entrance hall was lighting up the falling rain outside, against the darkness of the night. Mickey had gone.

Sometimes these hard drinking, rough and tough men could be very different, and seemed to need to talk. I remember one early evening; the Dog Man came to the door, begging for the usual sandwich. He was minus dog, and had a half full bottle of cider in his hand. I asked him to wait, and returned to the door a few moments later with the cheese sandwich I had made him. He took the sandwich, but made no move to walk away. In stead, his manner suggested that he wanted to talk. Well, the house was quiet, and several other workers were around, so I let someone know what I was doing, then stepped out onto the street, shutting the door behind me. He sat down on the pavement, leaning his back against the wall of the house. I sat down next to him. It was dusk, and apart from the occasional passing car, the road was deserted. The Dog Man politely offered me a swig from his bottle. Catching the faint aroma of surgical spirits, I politely declined.

Then he began talking about the life he used to have. He was once married, and in full time work. He had a daughter who was the apple of his eye, and his wife and daughter were his whole purpose in life. Then things began to go wrong. His wife began having an affaire with another man. His marriage came to an end, and his wife made it impossible for him to have any access to his daughter. As we sat there in the quietness, he told me of his efforts to get her to change her mind, and that it was now many years since he had any contact with his daughter – he didn't even know where she was living now. As he talked, I saw tears in his eyes, and within a short while, he was sobbing uncontrollably. I was beginning to understand what led a man to drop out of mainstream life, and to turn to the life of the homeless dosser alcoholic.

I heard several similar stories from other men during that time. The details were different for each, but the pattern was always the same. Each had built his life on something – a wife, a family, a business, a beautiful home, a respected social position, or something else – and that something had collapsed. As the foundations of life had crumbled, so had the man. Again and again I discovered that: so began the journey literally to the gutter.

I remember recalling the teaching of Jesus: **"Everyone who hears these words of mine and puts them into practice is like a wise man who built his house on the rock. The rain came down, the streams rose and the winds blew and beat against that house; yet it did not fall, because it had its foundations on the rock. But everyone who hears these words of mine and does not put them into practice is like a foolish man who built his house on sand. The rain came down, the**

streams rose, and the winds blew and beat against that house, and it fell down with a great crash." (Matthew 7: 24-27, NIV)

On more than one occasion, I realised with a shudder how close I had come to building my life on material things, on status and career, and thanked my God that He had seen fit to come looking for me, at a time when I was certainly not looking for Him, and to rescue me from a life that was fundamentally pointless and ill-founded.

There were other moments of drama too. Residents at the house were expected to sign on for benefits if they were unemployed, and to ask that the rent they were required to pay should be sent separately from their personal giro, in the form of a rent voucher. This was a useful way to ensure that the rent money, which paid for food and other items, was actually paid! Occasionally, a new resident would deliberately avoid making this request, and the giro he received by post would include the part of his benefit intended to cover the rent. The rule was simple: if a resident was two weeks in arrears with his rent, he was asked to leave, and this was made clear to every resident when he arrived.

On one occasion, a resident had accumulated two weeks' rent arrears. I really cannot remember his name, but I can see him in my mind's eye as I write this; he was a tall, balding man in his thirties, wearing a somewhat battered light brown leather jacket. Following the usual procedure, I phoned the Social Security office to ask about this, and was told that he had been paid all of his benefit in the form of a giro, for each of the two weeks for which he had claimed benefit while living at the house: he had not asked for a rent voucher.

A rule of the house was that residents must return by 10.00 pm. (This helped to reduce the number who returned very drunk.) The resident had not returned by that time. We workers surmised that he was now well aware that he had now failed to pay two weeks' rent, and that he would therefore be evicted if he did come back. We decided that he was very unlikely to return.

Residents and the other workers had all retired to bed by 11.00 pm. I was left alone in the office, because it was my turn to do 'night duty', as part of the fire precautions. At around 11.30 pm there was a ring at the doorbell. I opened the door (on the chain, just in case it was the heavy gang) to find the resident standing outside. I expressed surprise at seeing him there, as he knew that he could no longer stay at the house because of the rent arrears, and told him he would have to go. "I know", he said, "But can I come in for a few minutes first?" He asked with such pathos that I relented, and allowed him to come in. He told me that he hadn't eaten all day, and I made him a sandwich. He was doing everything possible to delay the moment when he would have to leave, but finally the moment came, and I asked him to go.

He took a razor out of his pocket, and looked me in the eyes. "I'm not afraid to use this, you know," he said. I asked him, as calmly as I could, who he was proposing to use it on, him or me? "I wouldn't hurt you, son," he said. "It's for me." He placed the blade in the palm of his hand, and begun to close his hand. "Look", he said, "The blade's bending under the pressure." Although I was young and inexperienced, I could recognise moral blackmail. Still, I had no idea how to respond to it. I put on my best sympathetic face, and said seriously, "Well, if you have decided that's the best way, I think you should have the right to do it. I certainly won't try to deprive you of that right. So I'm going to leave you alone in the office with that blade. I'll be back in five minutes." Then I left the office.

You may imagine that the next five minutes passed very slowly for me, pacing the floor, wondering whether I had made the right judgement call. After five minutes, I returned to the office to find the man still sitting there. He looked up at me and tried – not very successfully – to look like someone who had just made a major life-changing decision. "I decided it's not worth it", he said. I told him he should now leave. "I'm refusing to leave", he said quietly.

This happened frequently when a resident was asked to leave. If he just obligingly walked out, the man would lose a lot of status with the other local dossers. The responses that each of us would make so that this man could save face and reputation were as fixed as the steps of a line dance. I told him that, if he was refusing to go, my job was to call the police to witness his eviction. I also invited him to tell me if he was intending to prevent me making the call. He assured me that he would not stop me making the call, and sat quietly by the phone while I did so. The police were very busy that night, and told me that they would not be able to attend for about half an hour. No problem, I said. The two of us sat and chatted while we waited. The policeman finally arrived, and I formally asked the man to leave in front of the officer. He formally refused. The constable told him he had to go. He went. Now he could hold up his head in the local dosser community, as someone who had to be forcibly evicted by the police.

After we had been some time at Cambridge Cyrenians, one of the committee of local people that ran the administration of the project suggested that it would be useful for us to get some experience of other Cyrene projects. We readily agreed. Soon after this, it was arranged for Maggie to spend a fortnight at Exeter Cyrenians, at a project that was, like ours, a short-term house, in this case combined with an adjoining night shelter for homeless. We spoke several times by phone during her stay there. She seemed to have some reservation about the Exeter project, though I really could not work out what it was; Maggie couldn't put her finger on it, either. Unlike our Project at Cambridge, Exeter Cyrenians had a full time paid Project Leader. This was the first time I had heard that such posts existed within the Cyrenians, and I wondered a little whether our future might be with such a project.

One day, Maggie phoned me. It was the day after her day off. Having nowhere else in particular to go, she had spent her day off exploring Exeter town centre. (There was little point in spending the time hanging around the project, as she would inevitably end up working.) As she wandered round the town, she was stopped by someone she later described as "a funny looking hippie chap". He had curly hair, and was wearing jeans and a caftan. He asked her if she knew where he could buy a notebook. Maggie explained that she was a stranger to the area, and suggested that he might look for a branch of Woolworth's. Some time later, she encountered the young man again. He smiled, and said, "We meet again!" Maggie made some non-committal reply. After looking puzzled for a moment, the young man said to her, "Do you know the Lord?" (That's Christian slang for "Are you a Christian?") When Maggie said she did, the young man grinned, "I thought so," he said. "Come with me, there are some people you should meet."

When Maggie tells this story, she usually remarks that she was not in the habit of going off with strange men! On this occasion she did, and was taken to an amazing house: a large house, with many young people living in it, in the Pinhoe areas of Exeter. All of them were Christians, and the house was one of several owned by the Pinhoe Fellowship. This had originally been a small Church, meeting in the homes of members, but had grown far too large for any private home. Some of its members lived in houses owned by the Fellowship, while many other members lived in their own accommodation. On a Sunday, they all met together for worship in a large church building in the town. It was clear that Maggie was very impressed indeed by the brothers and sisters she had met there, and she spoke enthusiastically about them for some time on the phone. At the end of the fortnight, Maggie returned to the

Cambridge Cyrenians, and life returned to normal – inasmuch as there was any such thing as 'normal' in the project.

Some weeks later, one of the Cambridge Cyrene committee told us that the project leader at Exeter had just resigned, having taken a job elsewhere. Exeter Cyrenians had contacted her, asking whether Maggie and I might be prepared to work temporarily at Exeter, as they had no one to act as project leaders, pending the appointment of someone new. It was suggested that we would work for some six or eight weeks at Exeter, and then return to Cambridge. Particularly as I had been wondering about our longer-term future (one can only remain a full time volunteer for so long, after all) I was easily persuaded to accept the suggestion, especially as the project leader's job at Exeter was to be advertised shortly. We agreed that I would travel to Exeter shortly, and that Maggie would follow to join me a couple of weeks later.

Chapter 3

Exeter Cyrenians

The Cyrene project at Exeter was housed in a large disused wharf – 'Gabriel's Wharf'. Within minutes of entering the building, I knew what it was that had caused Maggie to have reservations about the place. It was difficult to be precise, but there was something about the building and the people living and working in it that was subtly different. It was partly the way that people were relating to one another there – lots of aggression poorly disguised as banter, lots of bad humour at the expense of others who were usually not present at the time. Those were features that I could describe and reason about, but not really the problem. There was about the place a brooding atmosphere of evil I had never encountered before. At the time, I just dismissed such thoughts as fanciful. If I had such an experience of unease today, I would take it far more seriously.

The Project was actually two projects in one: in the same building there was a night shelter for homeless, and a short stay house. The two were separated by a door, which, as I remember, was kept locked. There were few residents in the short stay house (For some reason I never worked out, the word 'hostel' was never used in the Cyrenians) because of the acute staff shortage. I met the paid leader of the project, who was leaving the next day to begin working as a prison officer. The only other worker there was a volunteer. Soon after I arrived there I was told that this volunteer had originally been a resident at the project, and that he had been homeless when he had arrived there.

I did not find among these people anything of the idealism that had been a common feature of Cyrene workers at Cambridge. Their conversation was intensely cynical, and in general they never seemed to be prepared to believe good of anyone if there was some less charitable possible explanation for their actions. I do not remember any signs of humour, except unkind jokes at the expense of others. The same attitude seemed to have infected not only those in the house but also many of the regular users of the night shelter. Since that time, during my years as a probation officer, I have worked with murderers and muggers, rapists, drug dealers and child molesters. Many of those have been people getting by the only way they knew how. Many of those were able to be charming or considerate, and capable of great kindness. I have never met with such unrelieved darkness in any group of people, before or since, as in that group of people at the Cyrene project at Gabriel's Wharf. I will say little about the details of the project, because there is much that is not edifying or helpful, either to me, or to the reader of this book.

Happily, by 'coincidence' (of the sort so unlikely that only the very naïve would think it was by chance) I had support in that situation. Maggie had made contact with the Pinhoe Fellowship, so it was easy for me to make contact with them again, and to introduce myself. This I did within days of arriving. So there were several houses full of Christian brothers and sisters to which I could go, and spending even a few hours at one of the Pinhoe Fellowship houses, enjoying the company of wholesome and loving Christians always felt like the mental or spiritual equivalent of a refreshing and cleansing bath after wallowing in a cesspit.

It was a great relief, a fortnight after I had arrived at Exeter, when Maggie came to join me from Cambridge. I was keen to hear news of the Cambridge project. One of the biggest changes concerned the resident Punch. Aware that the project was intended for short term residents, Maggie had one day asked Punch what his long term plans were, as he had already spent a long time living at the project. He had not given any clear response. The next day, Punch was gone. I absorbed the news with mixed feelings: Punch had been a strong influence on the house, and I could not quite imagine the place without him. On the other hand, he could also be very difficult, and had been from time to time a source of considerable difficulty to workers. I remember wondering at some length what effect this change might have.

Maggie's presence did nothing to relieve the oppressive atmosphere at Gabriel's Wharf, but it was wonderful to have again someone to relate to who was not caught up, seemingly obliviously, in the unpleasantness there. We both made a point of spending time, when we could, at the Pinhoe Fellowship, which made it possible to retain our sanity at least. While I would not wish for anyone the experience we had at Gabriel's Wharf, the contact with the Pinhoe Fellowship made our time in Exeter a time of great blessing and personal growth.

The Pinhoe Fellowship met together on a Sunday for worship in a large hall in the town. One of our new friends there introduced us to Jack Hardwich, A kindly and deeply spiritual man I guessed to be in his mid fifties, who, with his wife Daisy, was leader and pastor to the Fellowship. Jack suggested that we might like to come to a Sunday evening worship meeting of the whole Fellowship. We were able to take the time off, so we quickly accepted his invitation. Jack gave us some advice: "Not everything is helpful to everyone", he said, "So eat the meat and leave the bones – take what is useful and helpful to you from the experience." We both said that we would, and I secretly wondered what we would find there.

On that Sunday evening, we arrived at the worship meeting. Maggie was from a Roman Catholic background, and my only experience of Church was fairly ordinary Church of England, and this was certainly very different from anything we had ever experienced before. There must have been well over a hundred people gathered together. The joy in their worship was obvious: on their faces, in their singing, and in the naturally open and loving way they related to one another and to us.

The worship was led by guitars, and the hymns were what we would today call 'choruses' – lively songs of worship and praise with a modern beat – very commonplace now, but in 1974 still very unusual, and certainly new to us. I remember feeling filled with a wonderful sense of joy and love for God as we joined in the worship. Then suddenly, there was silence. Not orchestrated from the front, it just happened. In the silence, I heard the most beautiful sound; someone near the front was singing, in a foreign language. Then a few others began singing, harmonising, then more and more people. The singing was moving slowly through the crowd of people, closer and closer to us, moving like the waves of wind that blow over a cornfield. Then the singing was all around us. Many of those around us were on their feet, with real joy on their faces, singing, praising, many with their eyes closed, and with hands raised in prayer, and all singing in a language I didn't understand.

Suddenly, I seemed to be filled with love of the Lord, filled with an amazing joy; such love and joy I had never experienced before. Without really knowing what was happening, I was on my feet, with arms raised, singing joyfully to God, in a language I didn't know or understand. Tears of pure joy were streaming down my face.

For me, that was a wonderful evening, and a turning point in my life. Before that night, I had firmly believed that God loves me, and that my life is in God's hands. Since then, I **know** that He loves me, and I **know** that my life is His. The results of that night have stayed with me ever since, and the experience of praying in tongues has become a normal part of my experience of God. I had just had the experience that the Bible calls being baptised with the Holy Spirit, or being filled with the Spirit. (I should mention in passing that this was also a normal part of the Christian experience in the early Church, from the Apostles onwards, as the Bible makes very clear. See the book of Acts of the Apostles, chapter 2 and the chapters following for details of this. The experience, as described in the Bible, sometimes happened to a person at the time of becoming a Christian, sometimes as a separate experience, some time later.)

Jack and Daisy Hardwich had invited us to join them, the following evening, to go to a small prayer group they went to every week. They collected us by car, and took us to the meeting. The group met in a convent in Exeter. I guess that there were about ten or fifteen people there, and about half of these were sisters at the convent, wearing the traditional habit of nuns. There were no guitars, there was no hand clapping; we sat quietly in a small room, sometimes in silence, in an attitude of prayer. Sometimes one or another person in the room prayed out loud, often prayers of thanks and praise. Then there would be silent meditation for a time.

Several times, someone would open his or her Bible and read a passage. Several times, someone spoke into the silence, beginning what he or she said with "God says…" or "This is what the Lord says…" and I remember feeling quite certain that the living God had spoken to us through that brother or sister in the Lord. This is **Prophesy,** the speaking out of God's word, His specific message into a specific situation, to specific people – often to those listening. The Bible lists prophesy as one of the supernatural gifts of the Holy Spirit in I Corinthians 12. A few times, someone would begin quietly singing a chorus, and others would join in. The sense of God's presence was so strong I felt I could almost reach out and touch Him.

On the way home afterwards in Jack's car, all four of us were sometimes talking together quietly, sometimes silently enjoying the wonderful 'peace, which passes all understanding'. When Jack stopped the car for Maggie and me to get out, I remarked on how different this group was from the exuberant, joyful praise we had experienced the night before.

Jack turned to me and quietly spoke. **"David,"** he said, **"Always remember – the Spirit of God is a Spirit of infinite variety."**

Those words have stayed with me ever since; they are as clear in my mind today as on the evening they were spoken. Even though Jack did not start by saying "The Lord says…" I knew that I had just heard God's word to me personally. It was an important piece of teaching. A word of prophesy to me…

Those using the Cyrene project at Exeter had in common with those at Cambridge the fact that many would play 'mind games', trying to disturb or upset each other, or the project workers. On one occasion, for example, shortly before Maggie had joined me, I had been kept up very late indeed, attending to some row or disagreement between residents. I had finally got to bed, exhausted, in the early hours of the morning. At 5.00 am, after a very few hours sleep, I was awoken by the telephone ringing, on the table next to my bed. With real difficulty I roused myself from a deep sleep and answered the phone, wondering what emergency had happened. It was the telephone operator. Someone had booked an alarm call to that number.

New users of the night shelter at Gabriel's Wharf were arriving all the time. Each evening, we would make a large amount of soup or stew, and take this with several loaves of bread into the shelter for those who had arrived. One evening, one of the new arrivals told me he had just travelled to the town from Cambridge, and that he had spent some days as a resident at the Cyrene house. I was delighted, and asked for news of the place. He asked my name, then smiled and said he had heard of me.

He told me that there had been a meeting at Cambridge, and it had been decided that Maggie and I were no longer welcome to work there. I was sure that this was another 'mind game' and did not even consider the possibility that the organisation that had taught me the importance of open discussion and talking problems through would behave in such a way, deceitfully, behind our backs. As soon as I could, I phoned Cambridge to check. To my surprise and dismay, the news was completely correct. In being instrumental in causing the resident 'Punch' to leave, Maggie had apparently offended several members of the committee, who had regarded him as one of the (very few) clear success stories of the project. We could return, I was told, to stay as long as we needed to, at another house in Cambridge used by Cyrene workers during their time off, but we were no longer welcome to work there.

This was a blow I had never expected. We had sold our home and given up our jobs to work there, and the stay at Exeter had only been planned as a short-term task. I really had no idea what we were to do next.

Meanwhile, we had the continuing task of running the Exeter project for a little longer. Interviews had been held for the post of Project Leader, and the new appointee was due to take over in a few weeks time.

One day, on our day off, we had been invited to stay overnight at one of the Pinhoe Fellowship houses, in Heavytree Road, Exeter.

We had enjoyed a wonderful day of fellowship with some of those living there, and a group of us were chatting in the lounge in the evening. We were not the only guests there. One of those living in the house was a young woman who had become a Christian soon after a short and disastrous marriage had ended in divorce a few years before. Entirely by coincidence (?) she had encountered her ex-husband in the shopping centre, and the two had begun talking about what had happened to them since. She had talked enthusiastically about becoming a Christian, and about the Pinhoe Fellowship, and had invited him to visit the house at which she was living. He was visiting that evening, not for the first time, and was one of the group chatting in the lounge. As the hour grew late, people left the group to go to bed. Maggie went to the room we had been given, and I said I would join her later. Finally, only the young man and I were left. We chatted quietly about the house, and our impressions of the Pinhoe Fellowship.

He had been deeply impressed by the people he had met during his visits to the house, and by the love and peace that he sensed there. "They definitely have something I haven't got, and something I really want", he said. "I've really worked at this. I've read the Bible, I've talked with lots of people about it – but I just can't find it in me to believe!" I sat for a moment, thoughtfully absorbing what he had said. Suddenly, there came to mind a story Jesus had told about guests arriving at a man's home very late at night; he had no bread to give them to eat. He knocked the door of a neighbour, but the neighbour and his family had gone to bed, and the neighbour called from the window that he couldn't help. But the man just kept on knocking, and in the end the neighbour got up and gave him what he needed. Jesus taught that we should pray like that. I knew what to say. I turned to my companion.

"If you really want to believe, then I want you to give me a promise".

"What's the promise?" he asked, suddenly interested.

"I want you to promise that you'll spend two minutes a day on your knees, asking for the faith you're wanting. It doesn't matter how silly you feel doing it, or how certain you are that you're talking to yourself, the promise is that you'll go on doing that faithfully, until the prayer is answered".

Now it was his turn to become thoughtful. The remains of a coal fire glowed in the grate. Earlier in the evening it had been burning warmly. He stared into the last glowing embers thoughtfully for several minutes. Then he lifted his eyes to mine. Sometimes, eye contact means little or nothing. Sometimes, when you meet a person's eyes, you know that you are communicating soul-to-soul, spirit-to-spirit, like the way he looked at me now.

"I'm going to do that", he said, "I'm giving you that promise". Soon after that, I went to bed, and he left the house to return to his own home.

As it happened, I never met the young man again, but a few weeks later, shortly before we left Exeter, a message from him was passed to me by a member of the Fellowship: he had found the faith that he had been seeking, and was due to be baptised the following Sunday.

The fourfold Cyrene rule, universal among Cyrene projects, I had always assumed was known and accepted by all at the Exeter project. One day, we returned to the project, which we had left in the charge of the worker I have already mentioned, who had previously been a resident. In one of the communal rooms was one of the few residents of the hostel part of the project. He had a bottle of cider in his hand, and it was clear from his slurred speech that he had been indulging freely. I knew what had to be done. I asked him to leave. He argued that I was being unreasonable, and that he should be given another chance.

In my experience – very limited at the time – the fourfold Cyrene rule was the only thing that made it possible for a project to continue, and I felt that I had no choice other than to enforce it, unless, as acting project leader, I was myself to effectively disobey the 'rules of the house'. I was adamant that he should leave. He refused. I told him that I would need to call the police to witness an eviction. He said carry on. I phoned the police, and they duly arrived a short while later, and escorted the resident and his belongings off the premises. As he left, he asked one of the police officers if they could give him a lift to somewhere. He refused, and once he was on the public road, and no longer on Cyrene premises, the police left.

Over the next few hours, the man continued to hang around the surrounds of the building. He would occasionally shout abuse from the road, and was obviously getting more and more drunk. Finally, after dark had fallen, he began to try to break into the building, shouting increasingly murderous threats against me. In Cambridge, an event of this kind was always accompanied by a real closing of ranks by both residents and workers. To my horror and dismay, I found that, with the exception of Maggie, no one was prepared to offer support of any kind. The house was under siege, and those within it simply did not want to be involved. I really did not know what to do next.

I think it was the sound of breaking glass that finally enabled me to decide: if my presence here was the likely cause of the destruction of the project, then the best I could do for the project was to leave it. I phoned one of the members of the committee, a senior probation officer of many years experience, to discuss the situation.

He agreed that I should leave. I must say that, to this day, I find very surprising the complete lack of support I received from this senior and very experienced man. He had received a phone call from a very young, very inexperienced and very temporary project leader at his wits end, in a house that was effectively being besieged by a drunken and violent man nursing a grudge. There was no offer of real support, no offer to come down to the project, and no offer to send anyone else, or otherwise to assist. I was on my own.

I phoned my parents – the only people I could think of who would offer us a bed for the night and a place to go at such short notice. I explained the situation to my worried and concerned mother when she answered the phone. At the end of the call, while my mother in Chelmsford began making up the spare room to prepare for our imminent arrival, Maggie and I began to pack our few belongings. Police had to attend again to locate our besieger in the darkness. His rage had not abated. As we walked to the waiting taxi he was struggling furiously to get at us, and two large police were working hard to restrain him. It was with a sense of relief that we finally boarded the train to take us to Chelmsford. We wondered what the future had in store. I wondered whether I had got it completely wrong, or whether the Lord could possibly have let us down completely. I remembered the verse in the Epistles: "If we are faithless, He is faithful, because He cannot deny Himself".

In retrospect it is easy, with close to thirty years of experience working as a social worker, a residential worker and a probation officer, with clients who have included many violent and dangerous men, to see the mistakes I made then. It is also easy to look back and to see the hand of God preparing us for other things. Certainly, to have known that project at Gabriel's Wharf, and to have been touched by the brooding and malicious spirit that seemed to permeate the very fabric of the place was a learning experience never to be forgotten. Some years later, when I heard that the building had been demolished, I well remember feeling that the world was a better place as a result. By contrast, when I heard that the Cyrene building in Cambridge had been demolished, I felt a real sadness, as though a place where I had grown up was no longer there.

Chapter 4

Back in Chelmsford

When we had sold our house, following God's leading, and gone to the Cyrenians, there had been a certain sense of romance and adventure that, as a young man, I had found intensely appealing. The next few weeks, during which Maggie and I lived in my parents' spare bedroom, the atmosphere was one of anticlimax and disappointment. What were we to do next?

Well, the first thing was to find work, and somewhere to live. My mother and father were very kind, but living in someone else's home after being accustomed to our own space was not easy for us, and having us there was not easy for them. I think that all four of us learned new tolerance and self-control during that time. I had never been unemployed before, and queuing up for benefit was a new and difficult – not to say humiliating – experience.

We were unemployed and effectively homeless for a total of around ten weeks, and more than once during that time I found myself wondering whether God had deserted us.

I spent endless hours scanning the papers for work, and attended several interviews without success. Finally, I was offered a job working in the offices of a Finance Company. They called me a 'trainee manager', but the title meant very little. The work, from week to week, was either processing new applications for loans, or chasing those who, having borrowed money from the company, had defaulted on the repayments. So most of the time, I was either part of the process of persuading people to take out loans, or part of the process of persuading them to repay them, often on the doorsteps of their homes.

Meanwhile Maggie had gone back to working as a nurse, and the hospital offered us a staff house to live in. We moved into the furnished house soon after. The house had previously been let unfurnished, so we had the pleasant task of setting up a beautiful house, full of new furniture still in packaging from the shop. Maggie was thrilled, and pointed out to me that we gave up a house and furniture when we had gone to the Cyrenians, and now God was providing brand new furniture and an even nicer house to live in. Some months later, we took out a mortgage and bought a house again in Chelmsford. Things were looking up. I was buying social work journals every week, and applying for every advertised post for which my meagre experience qualified me. The house was smaller than the one we had been renting from the hospital, but more than adequate for our needs, and while the furniture we bought to go into it was mostly second hand, it was nice to feel that we had our own place again.

Meanwhile, through our connections with the local churches, we discovered Church House Trust. This Organisation, run by the Anglican Church, had a series of houses for what were described as 'mixed problem groups', including recovering heroin addicts, dry alcoholics, difficult children in care, and others. We also met the gentle and deeply spiritual leader and founder of that organisation, Tom Marriott. Middle aged, a little overweight and balding, with a mild and unassuming manner and a pair of thick-lensed glasses, he seemed somehow improbable as a dynamic Christian leader. And yet this man had started and was leading a Christian project that included seven or eight houses or hostels – old rambling vicarages made available by the Church of England, run by paid staff, financed by the church, ministering to the needy.

A perpetual problem for Church House Trust was enabling staff to get time off – since the residents of the houses were mostly far too dependant to be left without staff in the building, and Tom responded to our offer of help with real enthusiasm. So, at the end of each week of work, we would spend our weekends at one or another of the Church House Trust projects, taking over the running of the house so that the full time staff could take much needed time off, away from the stresses of their work. Slightly to our surprise, Tom also insisted on paying us for the work.

The work I was doing for the finance company was hard, demanding and boring, and the hours were long. I often returned home late at night, after working fourteen hours or more. From the beginning I had seen the job as a 'fill in' job – something to do until I was able to find a job in social work. I must have applied for a hundred jobs all over the country during that time, and attended a number of interviews without success. I would soon have been working for the finance company for a year. I was feeling increasingly discouraged.

It occurred to me that Church House Trust might well be the answer to my desire to move into a social work career. When Maggie and I met with Tom Marriott one day, I suggested that maybe God was calling us to work as full time staff there. Knowing that the project was permanently short staffed, I expected the suggestion to be met with enthusiasm. So Tom's answer surprised me. He became very thoughtful, then turned to us and said, "Well, let's pray about that. **There is only one Holy Spirit.** If God is calling you to work full time for the trust, we can confidently expect the same Holy Spirit to tell me that too".

This response surprised me, and also highlighted for me an important issue or **spiritual lesson.** Very often, I had head Christians talking about God's will as though it was negotiable, or as though 'I feel that God is calling me to...' was just Christian language for 'I want to...'

Looking back now, I know that I was using the words in that way. Tom's words showed me the difference between logical, pragmatic decision making (and there is nothing wrong with that) and the supernatural guidance God gives to His servants. The former would still make complete sense is a world in which there was no God. The latter **only** makes any kind of sense if there really is a supreme creator and sustainer of the universe, who really does have a plan for the growth, the development and the fulfilment of each one of His servants.

It was during lunch break one day working at the finance company that the breakthrough happened. There were a number of small rooms in which we would interview applicants for loans, meet with customers to sign papers, hand over cheques and so on, and I was sitting in one of these 'deal rooms', as we called them, eating my packed lunch, and mentally turning over my lack of success in finding a social work job. I wondered what God intended. We had heard correctly, I was sure, when He had called us to the Cyrenians. Now, He seemed strangely silent. I began half daydreaming, half praying, remembering those days when we had felt so sure that we were being called.

Suddenly, I woke from my daydream with a start. I knew what was wrong. In obedience to our Master and Lord, we had sold our home and gone to the Cyrenians because **He had called us.** What was wrong now was my own attitude. I was no longer surrendered to Jesus, no longer prepared to go wherever He led. I was not even really consulting Him – just repeating prayers that were little more than demands that he provide me with a career in social work. **While I was still calling Him 'Lord', I was treating God as if He was at <u>my</u> beck and call, instead of the other way round.** Something had to change. I remember wondering how I could really change, and avoid the self-deception at which I had always found it so easy to excel. Then I knew what I had to do. There was no middle ground. Either I was serving a miraculous God with plans for my life, or not.

I rested my elbows on the table in front of me, clasped hands together, and bowed my head in prayer. "Lord, we went to the Cyrenians because you called us. Now I've been trying to get into social work because of what I want, not because of what you want. I need to go back to being your servant. Lord, I'm going to stop trying to run my own life. I'm going to stop applying for social work jobs. I'm going to stop buying the journals where the jobs are advertised. You know how much I hate this job, but if you want me here till I retire, then I ask you to do that. I'm going to do nothing more about changing jobs until and unless you call me to other work."

Well, I have to admit that prayer gave me a definite sinking feeling. At that time, I was not even waiting to hear from any job applications. I had always treated the job I was doing as a temporary one. Now, I resolved to begin giving the job everything I'd got – to treat it as though it really was a lifetime career. I began to study in earnest the training units which, when completed, would earn me a promotion to a higher grade of work and salary in the finance company.

It was inevitable, given the number of social work jobs I had been applying for, that sometimes this had required me to be in more than one place at the same time. One example of this was an application I had made for the job of Assistant Warden at McIntyre House, a Probation Hostel in Nuneaton Warwickshire. They had invited me to interview for the post, but because of another commitment, I had not been able to attend. I had written to them, asking if I might be interviewed on another date, and they had replied, saying that no alternative date was available, and that they would consider that I had withdrawn my application.

A few days after that lunchtime prayer, a letter arrived on the doormat. McIntyre House was re-advertising the Assistant Warden post, and wrote to ask if I would like to reapply. After so many months of unfruitful job hunting, it seemed almost corny to imagine that God would respond so quickly to my change of attitude and renewed surrender, and yet, throughout the weeks between that letter and the interview date, I could not shake the sense of assurance that this was God's hand on my life, and that I would be successful at interview. Like many of the locations at which I had applied for jobs, Nuneaton was far too far from Chelmsford for me to commute. The post was an answer to our needs, however, because with the post was a self-contained two bedroom flat, within the hostel.

On the day of the interview I left home early, to begin the long train journey to Nuneaton. I had decided to treat myself, so I sat in the buffet car and enjoyed British Rail's best full breakfast, complete with waiter service, as I watched the world go by through the train window. The closer we got to Nuneaton, the stronger was the sense that this was indeed the Creator and Sustainer of the universe, taking a direct hand in my life. By the time I found the Hostel and knocked on the door, the sense of certainty was quite unshakeable. There were three other candidates, and after a tour of the hostel, the four of us were shown into the nicely furnished flat that would be the home of whoever was appointed.

I was the last to be interviewed, and the other three had each left without returning to the flat after their interview. Finally, it was my turn. I have only the haziest recollection of the interview that followed. I do remember that the panel consisted of the Warden of the Hostel, the Senior Probation Officer for Nuneaton, and the Assistant Chief Probation Officer for the area. For me, the interview passed in a daze. It seemed as though for every question they asked, the answer was already in my mouth, even for the difficult questions. In particular, I remember the question from the Senior Probation

Officer: "So, Mr. Carpenter you have some voluntary experience of residential work with the Cyrenians, but apart from that, you have no experience at all?" That had been true, of course, when I had first applied for the post many months before. Now there was Church House Trust to tell them about, and since Tom Marriott had insisted that we were paid a small amount for this, it was not 'just' voluntary work, either! I talked with some enthusiasm about Church House Trust, and as I did so, sensed a definite change in the atmosphere... questions after that were all warmly positive.

I was asked to wait in the flat for a few minutes, then asked to return to the room where the interview had been held. They offered me the job. For me, there was no sense of surprise, or relief, or triumph, just a sober acceptance that God, having enabled me to come to the point of real surrender during that lunch break at the finance company, was doing His will. I accepted the job with alacrity, and it was agreed that I would start work there after I had completed the period of notice required by my employers. The next stage of the adventure was about to begin.

Chapter 5

McIntyre House Probation Hostel

It was five in the morning, and I was woken by a knock on the door of our house in Chelmsford. I woke with a start, because I knew immediately who was knocking. It was the taxi driver, calling exactly at the time booked, to take me to the station to catch the train to Nuneaton, to finish moving the last of my belongings into the Assistant Warden's flat, and to begin work. I dashed to the door in my dressing gown, and explained to the waiting driver that I would need to ask him to wait for a few minutes. With a long-suffering smile he returned to wait in the taxi. Half an hour later, I was seated on the train, in the buffet car, enjoying another British Rail breakfast.

A few hours later, I walked into the Hostel, to begin my new job. Maggie was to continue her work at the hospital in Chelmsford until she was able to find a job in the Midlands, so, for the first time in several years, I was going to be living alone. Working in the Hostel was very different from any residential work I had done before. McIntyre House was run according to a strict regime by the Warden, a Deputy Warden, and one Assistant Warden – me. The other residential social worker was the Warden's wife, always referred to as Matron. The regime included strict times for residents to get up, to have meals, to go to bed. It also included a chores rota which the staff were expected to enforce, times by which residents must return to the hostel in the evenings, and a list of hostel rules – over 30 of them, as I remember – which were presented to each new resident as he arrived.

Residents, all between the ages of seventeen and nineteen, convicted of various criminal offences, would arrive at the Hostel for two weeks' 'bail assessment'. This meant that for this first fortnight on bail, the resident would need to follow the rules of the Hostel to the letter, or risk being returned to the Court at the end of the assessment period with a negative report, assessed as unsuitable, which would almost certainly mean that he would receive a custodial sentence. At the end of the two weeks, an assessment report to the Court was written by whichever staff member had been allocated as his 'keyworker', and a positive report meant that he would return to the Hostel with a two or three year Probation Order, with a twelve month condition of residence at McIntyre House.

I do not intend to say much about the day to day running of the Hostel. By today's standards it was very rigid indeed, regimented even. However, that was apparently the accepted way for a juvenile probation hostel to be run in those days, over thirty years ago, and anyway I was inexperienced, and considered that I was there to learn. I resolved to do the work as conscientiously as I could, to remain meticulously loyal to the warden, and to give the residents such understanding and care as they were able to accept. Nevertheless, working there was a constant strain.

Some weeks later, Maggie was able to find a nursing post in a hospital in nearby Leicester, and came to join me. We left the house in Chelmsford in the capable hands of a friend, a law student, who was delighted to have the opportunity to stay there at no cost, apart from paying the heating and lighting bills, and generally keeping the place aired and running so that we could return there when we had time off.

This was a particularly difficult time for Maggie. The flat was self contained, but our 'front door' opened onto the hostel first floor landing. Throughout the time we lived there, Maggie felt a little as though she was intruding every time she walked through the Hostel to get to the outside world, or to return to the flat after going out. This, and the stress of travelling to a place of work some distance from Nuneaton, using public transport, meant that Maggie was experiencing real stress. The strain we were both under began to affect our relationship, and we began to argue more and more. However, we were both determined to work through these difficulties. We contacted what was then called the Marriage Guidance Council (now called RELATE) and we were put on the waiting list for counselling.

During those weeks, we began visiting Churches in the area. We were exploring, to find out what Church we felt God intended us to join. Sunday-by-Sunday, we visited many. One of these was the local Pentecostal Church, where the worship was lively and joyful, and the members welcoming and friendly. One of these was Pauline. Some years older than we, Pauline still had a youthful manner, and a real enthusiasm and love for God. When she discovered that we were living at McIntyre House, and that I was a residential social worker, she began telling us with some excitement about someone called Malcolm.

It was clear from her description that Malcolm was really someone special. At the time when he became a Christian, he had a lengthy criminal record, and he had apparently become a Christian while serving a sentence in prison. Now, some years later, he was running Linkup, A Christian project with two hostels for homeless, one for men and one for women. Linkup also provided counselling for those in need of it, from a small office near the town centre. We heard that Malcolm was also a preacher and an evangelist. Pauline went on to tell us of large Church buildings filled to capacity to hear Malcolm preach, and of the many who had become Christians as a result of hearing him – one of whom was Pauline herself. She was quite insistent that we should meet Malcolm, and some weeks later we did meet him with his wife Jennifer at the Hostel for homeless women, which he and his wife ran at Oasten Road, Nuneaton.

Meeting with Malcolm was something of a surprise. The inspiring minister of God we had heard about had a manner that was mild to the point of self-effacing, and his voice was gentle and soft. We met for some hours, and I remember, as we told him about how God had led us through our adventures, and as he told us about how God had led him to establish Linkup, Maggie and I slowly realised that behind the mildness was real strength of spirit. I could well believe that the preaching of this gentle, softly spoken strong man filled Church buildings to capacity. Recalling other Christian ministers who had influenced us, especially Jack Hardwich and Tom Marriott, I recognised in Malcolm Worsley the same gentle, humble spirit that those men had shown. I recalled God's words to the apostle Paul with new understanding:

"My grace is sufficient for you, because my strength is made perfect in weakness." (2Cor. 12:9)

This was to be the first of many meetings with Malcolm and Jenny, and the two became good friends to us. Later, God was to minister to us through Malcolm to transform our marriage.

At that first meeting, Malcolm, hearing that we were looking to find the right Church for us to join, suggested that we visit St James Church, Weddington, a few miles from the Hostel. Since we had no car, this meant walking to church, but we were young and fit, and the next Sunday was a pleasant and sunny one. We arrived at the Church a few minutes before the service was due to start. Guy Cornwall-Jones, the minister of the Church, met us at the door and we told him our names. Slightly to my surprise he smiled and said, "Ah yes – Malcolm's friends". As we sat in our pew waiting for the service to start, Guy walked towards us with a couple about the same age as us, Bob and Judy Walker. He said to them, "Let me introduce you to some new friends". They sat next to us in the pew, and we began to chat quietly. Guy's words of introduction were accurate – they became firm friends of ours throughout our time at Weddington.

We also became friends with Malcolm and Jenny, and we visited them many times. I remember many evenings of chatting and praying together about events in the Church and events within Linkup. On one occasion Malcolm, aware that I was a residential social worker, told us that one of the real strains that he and Jenny were under was their inability to find time to be away from the project. There were others to look after the office in their absence, and the men's hostel could be left unattended. The real difficulty was finding someone to look after the homeless women's hostel in Oasten Road, where Malcolm and Jenny lived, and Malcolm asked if we might be prepared to help.

So began a more practically based connection with Linkup. From time to time, by arrangement, Maggie and I would be left in charge of the hostel for up to a week, and Malcolm, Jenny, and their two young children would go off for a well earned and much needed rest. We would simply take up residence there at those times, and I would go to the Probation Hostel to work my shifts while Maggie stayed at Oasten Road, then I would return to Oasten Road when my shift came to an end.

We learned a lot from our contact with Linkup, and with Malcolm. One evening we were visiting them in their front room at Oasten Road. We had begun marriage guidance counselling sessions, and I remember that we mentioned that to Malcolm as we talked. At the end of an evening, we would usually pray together for a short time before we left, and as that time approached, Malcolm asked if he could share with us a little of what the Bible says about marriage. We agreed, and waited expectantly.

Malcolm opened his Bible at Paul's epistle to the Ephesians and began reading at chapter 5, beginning at verse 22. **"Wives"**, he read, **"be subject to your husbands as to the Lord."** He looked at Maggie as he continued. **"For the husband is the head of the wife as Christ is the head of the Church, his body, and is Himself its Saviour. As the Church is subject to Christ, so let wives be also subject in everything to their husbands."**

Malcolm looked up at me from time to time as he continued to read. **"Husbands, love your wives, as Christ loved the Church and gave himself up for her that he might sanctify her, having cleansed her by the washing of water with the word, that He might present the Church to himself in splendour, without spot or wrinkle or any such thing, that she might be holy and without blemish."**

He turned to Maggie. "What that means, Maggie, is that you will answer to God for the way in which you are subject to your husband. He turned to me. "What that means, Dave, is that you will answer to God for Maggie's sanctification – for the way that you have nurtured her and enabled her to grow spiritually. She won't have to answer for your sanctification, but you will answer for hers." We talked about that briefly, prayed together for a few minutes, then we went home. Neither of us referred to Malcolm's words as we went back to the flat. I must say I felt it was a little bizarre in this twentieth century to expect a husband to take responsibility for the spiritual care of his wife like that – or to expect a modern wife to be subject to her husband. Anyway, Maggie would never agree to it.

After another few visits to the Marriage Guidance counsellor, she said to us, "I think you're alright now – you don't need me any more." We politely thanked her for her time, and began the drive back to Nuneaton in the van we had borrowed from a friend. We were both silent for a long time. Finally, Maggie blurted out, "What does she think she's changed?" Quietly, as I drove, I replied. "I don't know, love. Because everything's just the same, isn't it?" Maggie nodded in dumb misery.

A few days later, we had another row. I really can't remember what it was about, and nor can Maggie, but I do remember that we discussed for the first time that night the possibility that we might separate. We went to bed around midnight, with nothing resolved. Neither of us could sleep, and after we had tossed and turned miserably for hours, we got up again, made a drink, and sat in the lounge talking quietly, wondering what on earth to do next. Finally, Maggie said, "Maybe we should try to live together the way Malcolm said". We discussed the idea. It was amazing to me that Maggie would consider such an idea, but as we talked we both began to feel more and more positive. Finally, shortly before sunrise, we knelt together in prayer, and each of us made a commitment before God to live our marriage according to the scripture we had heard.

However I try to describe what happened next, it really doesn't convey even part of what we experienced. We looked at each other, feeling somehow renewed and revived, as though a great burden had been lifted from our shoulders. We hugged and kissed with real pleasure and real love, as we each realised that the other was experiencing the same thing. Then, slowly, we realised that we were very tired. We went to bed, and slept soundly. As I drifted off to sleep, I wondered whether our newfound optimism would have evaporated by the morning.

In the morning, it was still there, and we shared together excitedly how we both felt, as we ate a very late breakfast. Through easy times and hard times, that commitment we made and the underlying positive feeling about our marriage has been with us ever since. (It was only years later that it occurred to me that the word 'husband' actually means one who nurtures and cares for – so, for example, a book about plant husbandry is about caring for and looking after plants).

The other major influence during our time in Nuneaton was undoubtedly Guy Cornwall-Jones, the Rector of St James Church, Weddington, and his wife Helen. From that first meeting at the Church, both quickly became firm friends of ours. The Rectory was open house to the parish, and calling there, as we often did, we would often find other members of the Church, who had probably also called in 'on spec', for a coffee and a chat. We were members of St James Church for around five years, and during that time, Guy taught us many lessons about living out life as a Disciple of Jesus. Sometimes he taught us by talking, more often by his own gentle and unassuming example.

I personally benefited from Guy's positive influence, and particularly from the strong encouragement he gave me to develop and grow as a Christian minister. He was always very quick to point out that every mature Christian is a minister, and that the early Church was filled with ministers – prophets, teachers, evangelists and others, and that in the Church established by the apostles there was certainly not one man standing at the front every week, while all the rest sat passively receiving his ministry.

So when Bob and Judy, Maggie and I wanted to start a group, open to all, to meet regularly at Bob's home for prayer, Bible study and fellowship, Guy gave the idea his blessing, where many ministers might not have done so. The group began with four of us, and another man called Steve soon began attending. As we put out general invitations to all in the Church, numbers slowly grew. I must say that Guy's ability to trust that God was in charge, and that he

(Guy) really didn't need to be controlling everything that happened in detail was a source of great encouragement and growth for all of us. I believe that he only ever came to the group on one occasion, and that was because we specifically invited him. Over the course of the next year, the group grew larger and larger, until thirty or more were crowding into Bob's front room every Tuesday evening, and the group began discussing splitting into two smaller groups.

Maggie, while continuing to be involved in the Church at Weddington, had carried on attending mass each week at the Roman Catholic Church in Nuneaton. It was some months after our commitment to live our marriage according to scripture that Maggie asked me, one day, whether I thought that, in order to be properly subject to her husband, she should belong to the same Church. To me, this seemed like a wonderful idea. Still, the very fact that I was so pleased meant that it was difficulty for me properly to discern whether this was the prompting of the Holy Spirit, or just my own desire for us to be united in the same Church. We discussed the idea, and I said to Maggie that I felt that she should wait until she felt sure that this was what God intended.

The following week, Maggie returned from mass with excitement. Throughout the service, she had been filled with a certainty that she no longer belonged in the Roman Catholic Church. There was no longer any question or doubt in her mind — God was leading her to join me as a member of the Anglican Church. Some weeks later, at a brief ceremony at a service one Sunday, Guy and the whole congregation formally welcomed Maggie into the Anglican Communion.

Guy also encouraged me in another way, by suggesting that I should train as a Reader. For those not familiar with the Anglican system, I should explain that the order of Reader is a minor order within the Church. A Reader is first admitted to the Order by the Bishop, and then licensed by the Bishop to minister in a particular parish. He/she can lead most services, preach sermons, and has several other privileges, like being allowed to read the gospel reading at communion services. I was very uncertain about this idea, but Guy's encouragement, and the gentle prompting I felt from the Holy Spirit, finally led me to take the matter further. I began the fairly demanding training in scripture, theology and other things, and, some two and a half years and many written and other assignments later, was licensed as a Reader by the Bishop of Coventry, at Coventry Cathedral.

Some time after we had joined St James Church, we decided, after prayer, that we should sell the house in Chelmsford, and buy a house in Weddington. Our little house in Chelmsford was soon sold, and we bought a beautiful large house with four bedrooms in Weddington. It seemed amazing to us that God would provide such a big and beautiful place for us. Because of the difference in house prices between Chelmsford near London, and the Midlands, we moved from a little mid-terraced house in Chelmsford to a beautiful house which actually cost us less than the house we had sold.

At that time, Malcolm and Jenny were leaving Linkup, and another couple, Dick and Muriel, had been appointed to take their place. Dick and Muriel would be leaving their previous Christian work, and the accommodation that went with it, some seven or eight weeks before Malcolm and Jenny were leaving Linkup, and would need somewhere to stay during that time. As we heard Guy telling us about this, we felt the gentle prompting of the Holy Spirit, and we knew what out beloved Lord and Master was telling us to do. No wonder God had led us to so large a house.

The house did need rather a lot of decorating, and if Dick, Muriel, and their three teenage children were going to move in, it would need doing far more quickly than we had planned. To our surprise and delight, several members of St James Church told us that they felt God's call to help with this, and over the next few weeks a dedicated band of Christian brothers and sisters sanded, painted, hung wallpaper, and even fitted a new radiator in the lounge. A very few weeks after we bought the house in Weddington, all the work was completed, and Dick, Muriel, and their children moved in with us.

Malcolm went on to train as a Probation Officer, and at one point was even working as a Probation Officer at a prison at which he had once been an inmate. For details of this exciting story, see the book that has been written about his life – "Out of Bounds", by Judith Wigley, Published by Highland. I can recommend it – a really good read!

Dick and Muriel stayed with us for many weeks before moving into the house at Oasten Road. They were the first of a series of people – some Christian, some not – who stayed with us because of need, during our time there. Sometimes, the need was just for accommodation. Sometimes the need was for considerably more, and both Maggie and I spent many hours listening to some of the very difficult times and experiences of those who stayed with us. The house was also 'open house' to the Church, and often I would come home from a shift at work to find an assortment of friends at the house – one or two currently staying with us, and others, members of the Church, who had just dropped in for a coffee and a chat.

One day a friend of ours, a young married woman in the Church, phoned to ask if she could come round to discuss a problem. When she arrived, she told me about the terrible way that she felt her faith had been damaged, during the part time psychology course she was doing at the local college. The lecturer, an atheist, had spent some time discussing human needs, and then showing the way that

Christianity fulfilled them. He argued from this that Christianity was just an invention by inadequate human beings to fulfil their own needs. She found her faith terribly shaken, and after some weeks without peace, had come to see me.

As I listened to her obvious distress, I began to wonder why it was that my own study of psychology had not caused me similar problems. Actually, that was not quite the right question: the right question was not why, but **how** I had studied psychology without experiencing it as a major assault on my faith. I realised that I had always used the psychology I had studied as a tool to do to the best of my ability the work that God had given me to do. In this way, I was putting man-made psychology in its rightful place, as one of the tools I used to serve my Master – in other words, I had used my faith to put psychology in its right place.

What that lecturer had done was doing was basically invalid – he was using man made psychology to try to understand the creator of the universe – effectively putting psychology above God himself. That was effectively idolatry, and had led to illogical and invalid conclusions – the very mode of argument assumed the non-existence of God in order to prove it.

After our friend had gone, I found myself feeling worried or burdened about her. I prayed long and earnestly, asking God for His healing in the situation, and surrendering our friend, and the outcome of the situation, into God's care. Then I got on with other things. Some weeks later, we met our friend again at a Church event. She asked me whether I had been praying for her after that meeting – she had felt a powerful sense of the presence and the love of God, and a conviction that someone was praying for her, as she had travelled home after our meeting. She had also found complete freedom from the problem that had been oppressing her.

We had now been married around seven years. Although we had always intended to have children at some time, somehow the time had never seemed right. I must say that I was not in any great hurry, and I guess that it was easy to keep on putting off the moment of decision. Then one day Maggie brought up the subject in conversation. I think I made some non-committal response about having children one day. Maggie turned to me with absolute conviction, and said to me, **"David, I want a child."** Sometimes there are moments when it is good to recognise the irresistible force. It would have been pointless to argue, and while the thought of a baby and managing on one income was daunting, it also seemed very right and easy to surrender the future to God. Secure in the knowledge that we would only conceive if God intended it, I agreed. So it was that a little over nine months later, our son James was born.

Any man who has been present at the birth of his child knows that the experience is a profoundly moving one. Others had told me horror stories about blood, and strong men passing out at the experience. What no one had prepared me for was the deeply emotional aspect of the experience. As I watched our son coming into the world, I continued to comfort and encourage Maggie – who, after all, was the one doing all the work – but actually, I could hardly see, because my eyes were streaming with tears. I have rarely felt such total joy. If any man reading this is considering whether or not to be present at the birth of his child, I can only say that it is an experience I will never forget, and I am so glad that I was present. I phoned my parents and Maggie's parents with the news. By the end of each telephone conversation, they were in tears too. Both sets of new grandparents visited Maggie in the hospital soon after.

Then, some days later, mother and baby were discharged, and we were together again in our home, with our new son.

It was, for us, a strange experience having our son home with us. We both felt very aware that we were now responsible for this new human being, who was depending on us for the things he needed to survive and grow. We both felt the experience was slightly unreal, as though any moment the parents of this baby would arrive to take him back. We kept realising again that the baby's parents were us, and that he was here for good...

Our many brothers and sisters in Christ continued to visit us often at our home, and we continued to make them welcome. To start with, our new family member made little difference to our involvement in the Church: he was a remarkably good-natured child, and would contentedly sleep in the carry-cot in the corner of the room, while we met in a fellowship group, or attended some other Church meeting. Even the inevitable broken nights when our son just wouldn't sleep seemed a small price to pay for the pleasure and happiness his presence brought us, and while we could still be grumpy in the mornings after a sleepless night, it was easy to laugh at ourselves for our bad moods.

The life at Weddington seemed so good it seemed as though it would go on forever. Working at McIntyre House was a frequent source of stress, but it was easy to leave that stress at work, and every spiritual diet needs a little roughage. One day, my parents were visiting us at our home. We were chatting in the evening, after putting James to bed. Then my mother asked me when I was going to get a better job. I remember reacting quite badly to that question – probably because, at the back of my mind, I knew that just remaining an unqualified residential social worker was going to make it difficult or impossible to provide well for our new son, and I had been putting off thinking about that.

I had, for some years, been wondering about the ordained ministry in the Anglican (Church of England) Church. I had gone to a selection conference some years before for selection for training. The conference recommendation had been, 'not yet recommended for training'. This, I was told, was a clear invitation to attend another selection conference later. However, this was not to be an immediate possibility, and when I had subsequently met with the Bishop, he had encouraged me to consider training in some other work in the meantime.

At the time, this had seemed a great disappointment. Now, I am so grateful for the wisdom shown by the selectors at the conference, and by the Bishop when I met with him. I was certainly not cut out to be a parish vicar, and I now know that, had I tried to be, the results would have been disastrous. I was also learning, through all of this, that God often moves a lot more slowly than we might want Him to (specifically more slowly than I want Him to!) and that it is only when we really surrender to Him as Lord of our lives, and our greatest desire is to serve Him in whatever way He chooses that we can really experience the wonderful victorious life of the disciple of Christ.

After several years as a Christian, it may seem to you surprising that I needed to learn again this elementary lesson. Somehow, it was so easy, while paying lip service to an all-powerful Lord who holds the lives of His disciples in the palm of his hands, to think and act as though it was all up to me, and as though it would all go wrong if I didn't organise it. Visiting Guy and Helen one day, I was reading their calendar, which had a short daily meditation. The meditation was about God's guidance, and said something that I had not heard before – if there is no clear guidance from God, *it means don't do anything different, carry on as you are.*

So when my mother asked that question, it struck something of a raw nerve. Still, over the weeks that followed, the question stayed with me. At that time, a friend from the Church was staying with us. She had recently completed a degree at university, and was now in the process of finding out about doing further, vocational training. It was as though everything around me was steering me in the same direction. I began to feel the familiar, sometimes uncomfortable nudging that I was coming to recognise as the prompting of the Holy Spirit. Others in the Church whose wisdom and spiritual maturity I respected felt that seeking further training might well be appropriate, and that even included the advice of a Bishop! I began to think and pray earnestly about it, and some weeks later began the process of applying for training for professional qualification as a social worker.

Chapter 6

Moving On

It soon became clear that neither my current employers, nor any other social work agency was likely to provide any help for this mature student to train. Student grants were still available in those days, but they were set at a level intended to supply the needs of a young person without commitments. There was a small supplement for mature students, but the total I would receive was woefully inadequate for the needs of the three of us, including a growing son. After much prayer, we concluded that we should sell the house and buy something cheaper, to reduce as much as possible the size of the mortgage. A few months later, we moved from our large house on the (comparatively) nice side of Nuneaton to a small terraced house in Camp Hill – the other side of Nuneaton.

We also found that we had to change other aspects of our lifestyle more than a little, as we adjusted from living on a salary to living on a student grant. This can be described as an interesting experience. Very soon after I began as a social work student, it became clear that, despite our careful working out on paper, and despite our various economies, the grant was simply not going to be sufficient. So began the routine of working at college during the day, working at home preparing and typing assignments most evenings, and working at part time employment on other evenings and at weekends, to make ends meet.

After a short time as a taxi driver, I found part time work for a company selling cavity wall insulation, and during the time at college worked for them first as a sales canvasser calling from door to door, and later as a 'consultant', following up leads generated by canvassers, calling at the homes of interested potential customers, selling on a commission only basis. All the sales training I had received when working for the pharmaceutical company proved invaluable, and I soon developed a reputation with that company as an effective salesman. Later, I also worked for them at the National Exhibition Centre, staffing their stand at the Ideal Homes Exhibition. I enjoyed the work, and found selling on commission stimulating and challenging. This also allowed me to earn well, because I was often successful. Towards the ends of my training as a social worker, the company offered me a full time job, at a salary considerably more than I could expect to earn as a social worker for many years, and turning down that very generous offer was for me one of the harder tests of my preparedness to be obedient to God's calling.

During the time studying at Coventry, I do not think I picked up a fiction book or read a book for pleasure even once, because much time was needed to keep up with the consistently fast pace of the course, and because when I did have free time, the last thing I wanted to do was yet more reading! The course was based on concurrent placements: half of each week was spent in academic study at college, the other half working under a practice teacher in a social work agency. In the past, I had been accustomed to coasting much of the time, then cramming before exams. I could not do that here: the qualification was based not on examinations but on the successful completion of written assignments, each of which had a deadline. Each of four practice placements and every assignment needed to be passed to gain the coveted C.Q.S.W. (Certificate of Qualification in Social Work) at the end. To put it another way, just one failed placement or assignment was enough to prevent qualification!

My solution to the anxiety this generated for me was to work and work and work. Often, this meant arriving home in the evening from college or placement, relaxing for five minutes with Maggie, then going upstairs to work on assignments till one or two in the morning, pausing for long enough to eat the meal brought to me by my long-suffering wife. Needless to say, there was no time to continue ministering as Reader at Weddington Church, and after much prayer and discussion with Guy I decided not to ask for my licence as a Reader to be renewed, when the time came for this.

By the time I had finished working on assignments for the evening it was often very late, and Maggie had gone to bed. This was the time when Citizen's Band (CB) radio had recently been legalised, and several of our neighbours had CB radios in their homes. I decided to buy one, and soon found that listening and chatting to others on the CB was an interesting and absorbing way to wind down before bed. CB radio is pretty well unique. The range is very limited – probably a little over five miles. This means that the people you are talking to are members of the local community. This made a wonderful way to meet people in the area we had moved to, particularly as the local CB users had begun their own social club, meeting once a week at a local working men's club. So I got to meet many of those I had chatted to on the radio. Sometimes, after chatting to someone for a while, we would arrange an impromptu meeting, sometimes at the house of one of us, sometimes at some other location. In these ways, I soon got to know many in the local community.

One such contact, who became a good friend, was Dave Smith. A large, somewhat unkempt, bearded man, Dave lived a short distance from our home. He worked as a 'general dealer', which meant wheeling and dealing in any way that he could to earn a living. During the time I knew him at Nuneaton, he dealt in many different goods, from car roof racks to second hand washing machines – anything he could buy cheap and sell on at a profit. He had a dry, bluff manner, and I never once heard him pay a straightforward compliment to anyone. He was, however, a master of the backhanded compliment, and the dour exterior hid a gentle, caring nature, like a hard protective shell concealing a vulnerable creature.

Somehow, Dave and I hit it off immediately, and he soon became a regular visitor to our home. Occasionally, when I was taking an few hours off from college work, he and I would be sitting, discussing life, the universe and everything, till well after midnight. On those occasions, Maggie would usually join us for the early part of the evening, but she had always needed more sleep than I did, and would retire to bed when ready, leaving us to carry on putting the world to rights, over another glass of wine. Of course, Christianity was one of the subjects we sometimes discussed, and Maggie and I were always prepared to answer openly his questions about our faith. These questions often showed great thoughtfulness and insight. Still, both Maggie and I judged that it was wiser to avoid suggesting to this arch-individualist that he might make such a commitment for himself, although privately both Maggie and I remarked to each other that so gentle and caring a man would make a wonderful Christian.

At college, I encountered ideas very different from those I knew. One of the required subjects was called Social Policy, and the lecturer was very open about the fact that he was a committed Marxist, and a fully paid up member of the British Communist Party. He made some real effort to redress the imbalance that gave to his teaching, but the bias was very evident, nonetheless. This put me in something of a dilemma. The Marxist perspective is strongly atheist, and one I really could not accept. Since this lecturer would be marking assignments of the subject, should I write these in a way that meant that he would be reading what he (maybe) wanted to read?

The first Social Policy assignment I chose was an examination of the political, economic and structural causes of poverty in society, and after a brief struggle with my conscience I realised that I could only approach this by arguing strongly against the Marxist viewpoint. Since passing this assignment was essential if I was to remain on the course, I also decided that the assignment would need to be pretty close to bullet proof. (Reading this, you may feel that this showed some lack of trust in the professionalism of the marker – but this was one of my first assignments, and I wasn't about to take any unnecessary chances!) The experience of the Cyrenians had led me to feel very strongly about the issue of poverty, as you may imagine, and this strong feeling was increased by the practice placement I was doing at the time, working in a community work agency in the very poor and disadvantaged area of Hillfields, in Coventry.

So I began work in earnest to produce as unimpeachable a refutation of the Marxist viewpoint as I possibly could, thereby increasing my already heavy workload. In the process of researching and writing the assignment I was, of course, also working out my own ideas and opinions about the subject. Finally, it was finished, and I handed it in. I had argued as cogently as possible, and had backed up my arguments with as many unimpeachable authorities and as much research on the subject as I could find; I wondered how the marker would react to it. Many weeks later, the assignment was returned, with a mark of 'B+'. That was a good mark, but a long way short of an 'A'! Consumed with curiosity, I turned to the comments made by the marker: what criticisms had he made?

After reading with care his detailed comments, I realised that there were no criticisms at all. I discussed the mark with the lecturer, asking what more the essay needed to be worth an 'A'? He vaguely said that he had no specific criticisms, but "just felt that it was not quite the standard of an 'A'". I decided to appeal the mark to an external assessor, and was delighted when, some weeks later, the assignment was returned, upgraded to a straight 'A'.

Another very new idea was feminism. The reader will understand that many of the ideas that are commonplace now were very new then. I was not the only male student to struggle with ideas such as non-sexist language and other issues, which some of my female fellow-students would debate strongly during discussions on the subject. I remember what remarkable patience they showed, slowly educating us dinosaur males in what was then called 'the feminist perspective', and would now just be normal non-discriminatory language and behaviour.

It was also at Coventry that I first encountered the reality of racism in our society. Again, I have to pay tribute to several black students on the course, who patiently helped me to understand this. I had always known about the more obvious and overt examples of racism – racially motivated violence, for example. Now I began to understand that racism can be far subtler, and can even be the result of unconscious racism in white people who would be horrified to be thought of as racist.

For example, a black student called Gloria told me of an occasion when she had gone to the bank to cash a small cheque. She waited in the long queue of customers, many of whom were also cashing cheques. When it was her turn, she went to the cashier's window, and was asked to wait. A minute or two later, the cashier returned to the window, and asked how she would like the money. Gloria knew well that the cashier had just been to check that she actually had the money in her account before cashing Gloria's cheque. She had just watched a series of others cashing cheques with no such checking. All of those had been white.

Challenging such a small piece of discrimination might seem petty to many, but as Gloria pointed out to me, the cumulative effect of a thousand such small pieces of discrimination on the self-confidence of the normally sensitive individual can be devastating. Gloria asked the cashier what she had just been doing. When she was met with spluttering incoherence, she told the cashier the answer to the question, which both already knew. So Gloria asked the next question: why had the cashier seen fit to check her balance before cashing her cheque, when she had not done so with any of the other customers?

The cashier became even more incoherent, and appeared acutely embarrassed. Gloria pointed out that she was the only black customer in the queue, and that this was discrimination. She demanded to see the manager, and made a formal complaint. By happy chance, the victim of this racist attitude had been Gloria, a highly intelligent and articulate woman, secure in the knowledge that she and her husband had been good customers of the bank for many years.

She knew that, by challenging the racism she encountered, she was also working to improve the lot of many thousands of other black people who simply accept countless such subtle insults every day, because they are not articulate enough, or confident enough, to challenge them. Gloria was patient with me, and with many other white students who, like me, took some time to really understand the powerful way in which such subtle discrimination, repeated often enough, can be experienced as a major assault on the self-confidence and the self-image. So it was that, often, other students were at least as much my educators as the lecturers and practice teachers.

My greatest enthusiasm, however, was for studying those subjects that were directly about helping people, and especially subjects like counselling, human growth and development, and other aspects of psychology. Years before, my mother had trained as a Marriage Guidance Counsellor, and during her training she had often talked about what she was learning. I had always encouraged her to tell me more, because I had always found the subject interesting to the point of fascination. Now, for the first time, I had the opportunity seriously to study the subject. I felt like a kid let loose in a sweet shop!

I devoured voraciously textbooks about psychology, counselling and approaches to psychotherapy, adding to my already demanding reading list. Whenever possible, I chose assignment subjects that allowed me to concentrate on this aspect of social work. The largest piece of work was an extended dissertation to be handed in shortly before the end of the course. Most of my fellow students chose titles related to their favourite client groups – child abuse, elderly, and so on. My own enthusiasm for the psychological and counselling aspects of the work led me to choose something more theoretical: the subject of my extended dissertation was, 'Towards a Theoretically and Practically Integrated Cognitive Behaviour Therapy'. (The reader with psychological training will know that there is, nowadays, considerable connection between these two approaches to helping. As I write this, I am reminded that at that time, almost twenty five years ago, Cognitive Therapy and Behaviour Therapy were very separate approaches).

My recollection is of a time studying with all work and no play. However, this recollection cannot be quite accurate, because a few months before the end of the course, our second son was born. James was at this time a little over three years old. Maggie was admitted to hospital for the child to be delivered, and then promptly went 'off the boil'! She was discharged from hospital again, still heavily pregnant, and I remember going into college for an important group tutorial, while Maggie went for a *very slow* walk around Coventry. This caused some hilarity among other members of the tutorial group, and I recall one of my fellow students, grinning, shouting out of the window, "Keep yer legs together, Maggie!" Not that anyone could hear, as we were on the fourth floor.

The following day, Maggie went into labour again, I drove her to hospital, and Peter was born. A few months later, I qualified as a Social Worker, and the next chapter of our life began.

Chapter 7

Residential Child Care

As the end of the course came closer, I became progressively more aware of the fact that I had given up secure employment in order to train, and that, because I was not sponsored by any employer, the future was uncertain. It was all very well for lecturers and others to assure us that we would have no difficulty finding employment again – they weren't the ones with no job to return to in a few months time! It made sense to return to residential social work for several reasons. First, it was what I already knew. Second, it paid a little more than field social work. Finally, there had been many moments during training when I had looked back on this or that decision or action taken as a residential social worker and thought, "If only I had known then what I have just learned now!" For this third reason I was hoping to return to working with an age group similar to that of the clients I had worked with before qualifying – that is, late teens.

One of the first organisations to offer me an interview in response to my application was an organisation I will call Blankwater Community Home with Education (Not its real name). 'Community Home with Education' was the modern name for what had previously been called Approved Schools, and they housed many of the most difficult young people in care, including many who had been convicted of criminal offences. In many ways, the setting was idyllic – set in acres of rolling countryside, the dignified Victorian buildings looked more like a traditional public school than a home for difficult children in care. During one part of the interview with the headmaster (as the head teacher was called in those days) one of the young people knocked on the door of the study, and on being asked to enter made some request. His deferential and courteous manner impressed me, reminding me of the grammar school I had attended as a child. When I was offered the job of Deputy Housemaster, I accepted with alacrity.

It took only a few days of working at the school to realise that I had made a mistake. I was the only fully qualified person working at the school, and the small number of staff compared to the large number of young people meant that the regime was necessarily extremely regimented. Order was maintained by shouting, much in the manner of a drill sergeant, and by simply intimidating and bullying the young people into obedient submission. There were many very emotionally disturbed young people at the school, and the regime seemed to me to be designed to ensure that the emotional damage they had already suffered was compounded as much as possible.

The vast majority of the young people were boys between the ages of around thirteen and sixteen, and for these boys there was never any privacy from morning to night. (The few girls at the school lived in separate accommodation and, I understand, were treated somewhat better). A typical day began when the boys, sleeping in a dormitory housing around twenty, were woken, and queued up with their toothbrushes to each be given toothpaste from the tube by a staff member. Washing was in large communal washrooms, and each 'house' would then be shepherded by its duty housemaster to its houseroom, for breakfast.

The school uniform consisted of jeans, boots, and knitted nylon shirts. Since each house was only allowed to shower three times a week, all together in a large communal shower room, the reader can imagine that a group of twenty young men, sweating in nylon shirts that were changed only twice a week, were noticeably smelly by the time it was their turn for a shower.

Treat humans like animals and they will often begin to behave according to expectations. There were frequent outbreaks of fighting among the boys, and we staff were often standing between them to prevent it. Of course, with so many of them, and so few staff, it was inevitable that the fight would only be postponed, and would usually be continued somewhere else later. The staff simply continued to demonstrate to the young men the lesson that most had already learned in their homes before coming into care: control others by intimidating and bullying them, before they do the same to you.

In this inhumane setting, one of the few ways for a young man to escape from the misery for a few hours was to become intoxicated, and glue sniffing was a common pastime, whenever the opportunity arose; smuggling glue into the school after spending time on leave at home was commonplace, and was considered normal behaviour by many of them. Predictably the staff responded, not by attempting to improve the lot of those in their charge, but by enforcing a routine of showering, under the supervision of a staff member, on return from any period away from the school. This provided the opportunity to search all clothing, of course. This measure was fairly ineffective: young men would simply hide their glue in the grounds of the school before reporting back from home leave, and recover it later.

I had been at the school for about a month when I happened to be present when a large, intimidatingly muscular young man, with a snarl of anger, grabbed another smaller boy by the throat, pinning him against a wall. The pressure to the smaller lad's throat and the change in the colour of his face made me fear for his safety. A moment before, there had been several staff members around, but now, suddenly there was only me. I tackled the boy, who was large, muscular, and several inches taller than me, and managed with some difficulty to wrestle him away from his victim. As I pulled him away, we both fell to the floor, and the boy landed on top of me.

Other staff had now returned, and the lad was lifted off me. Someone asked me if I was all right. As I breathed in to reply, a searing pain in my rib cage told me that I was certainly not all right. I was taken to hospital for x-ray, and subsequently told that, although there were no broken ribs, I had torn badly the cartilage that connects the ribs. To my delight, I heard the examining doctor tell me that I would be unfit for work for many weeks to come.

It was clear to me that I would not be able or willing to continue to work for long at Blankwater School. Moreover, I felt that it might well be urgent that I leave very soon: another staff member at Blankwater had told me that the headmaster kept people from leaving by ensuring that any who applied for jobs elsewhere were given such poor references that they were unsuccessful.

During my month or so of sick leave, I contacted a Barnardo's project, the Druids Heath centre, which was also a Community Home with Education, to which I had first applied before being offered the job at Blankwater. While still on sick leave I was interviewed, and offered a job at the Druids Heath Centre. Before interview I spent two complete days at two different residential units within the Druids Heath Centre, and was delighted by the very professional and caring approach of the staff, the excellent staff to client ratios, and the quality of the care provided to the young people. I accepted the offered post, and it was with real pleasure and a great sense of relief that I gave to Blankwater School a month's notice of my intention to leave.

When I wrote the account of these events in the first draft of this book, I recalled that, a few weeks before, I had watched a news item on television. A senior staff member at Blankwater School, now retired, had just been sent to prison for a series of offences of abusing the young people there. I remembered him well from my brief time there, and wondered that I was so naïve that I never suspected this. Looking back, I recalled with a shudder a certain lurking sense of unpleasantness that hung over the place.

About the only thing that the Druids Heath Centre had in common with Blankwater School was the designation 'Community Home with Education'. Rather than being a large block school, the Druids Heath Centre consisted of a number of smaller residential units. The philosophy behind this was that by providing the services of a CHE in small units within the communities of origin of the young people, their links with those communities could be more easily maintained, so that their eventual return to their own communities could be made that much easier. So there were three residential units, one in Walsall, one in Sandwell, and one in the Woodcross area of Wolverhampton.

Each of these housed young people in care, referred to the Centre by the corresponding Local Authority Social Services Department. In addition, there was an Education Unit: a small purpose-built school with its own staff of trained specialist teachers, an Administration unit, which provided admin. facilities for the project, and a Family Placement Unit, which recruited, trained and supported paid specialist foster parents, called Family Placement Workers, for those young people who were not able to return home when they no longer needed the high level of structure provided by the residential units.

There was another residential unit, called the Alternative Care Unit. This was intended for short-term placements for young people from the residential units whose behaviour was so difficult or disruptive that it was temporarily impossible for them to continue living in the ordinary residential units. It was a locked unit, to provide a short time of stability, structure and security, to enable young people there to receive intensive work to enable them to change their behaviour, so that they could be returned to their own residential unit. It was as one of the staff in this Alternative Care Unit that I began working.

The contrast with Blankwater could not have been more marked. Because this unit was working with the most difficult young people in the Centre, the ratio of staff to young people at any one time was very high, and a very high proportion of the staff were trained and qualified. It was not unknown for there to be more staff on duty than young people resident, as the nature of the unit was that numbers varied, as young people would be returned to their units, to family placement, to their own families or to independent living as soon as their progress allowed this. At times the behaviour of young people there could be every bit as challenging as at Blankwater, but the combination of a small group and a high proportion of trained staff meant that such behaviour could be contained and worked with constructively, rather than just bullied into submission. Above all, no young person was ever just dumped at the unit, and left. From the moment a young person arrived at the unit, work began to return him or her to an ordinary residential unit or some other placement within the Centre. This was part of the larger plan: from the moment a young person was referred to the Centre by the local authority, work began to return him or her to the community.

At the Alternative Care Unit (called the ACU) there was, as one would expect, rather more structure than at other parts of the Centre. A very strong influence on the ethos of the highly professional working of the unit was the Principal Social Worker in charge of it, Steve Petts. A fit-looking, wiry no-nonsense man with a northern accent, he could seem as tough as nails when reprimanding one of the young people, but was tougher by far with any social worker who was shirking his or her duty to care to the best of his or her ability. Steve always made it clear that, whether he was on duty or not, he was likely to turn up at the unit at any time. When he did so, his first stop was always the office, to read the log. If he found any staff in the office, he would ask why, and if there were no legitimate reason, they would swiftly be sent to rejoin the young people – "Your job's with the kids, not the paper!"

Every young person in the unit had a Key Worker, who was responsible for preparing a detailed plan to ensure that the needs of the young person were being met, working towards an appropriate longer term placement. This meant that, although it was a locked unit, young people at the ACU had the hope and optimism that comes from knowing that you are working towards something better, and that it is achievable. You, the reader, will understand that following the experience of Blankwater School, the work at Druids Heath was a real blessing to me. During the time there, I had the opportunity to work with disadvantaged young people and their families, with skilled and expert support and supervision, in a way that made a real and positive difference to their lives. I also had the opportunity to use the training and skills I had acquired at Coventry, and to prove to myself that these really could make a difference to the lives of others.

One young man, John, was referred to the Centre by a local authority from further away, one that did not usually refer to the Centre. He was referred as a last resort, because the local authority simply did not have any facility able to contain him and work with him, because his behaviour was so difficult. He was in his early teens. He had a loving family, but they were quite unable to cope with him. In discussion with John, I devised a programme for him that included a behaviour modification programme – specified good behaviour earned stars entered on a star chart, which in turn earned privileges, including time out of the unit for specified activities, and in the later stages time visiting his family at his home. Some might think that such a programme would be harsh and inhuman. John certainly didn't think so – and neither did other young people at the unit, some of whom began assertively asking their keyworkers why they couldn't have a star chart like John's!

At the same time, I was working with John's family, and particularly with his mother. The plan was that John would ultimately return to live with his mother, once his behaviour was stabilised. I met with her frequently at her home, reviewing and adding to her parenting skills, and especially her ability to use effective and consistent methods to control the lad. She initially responded with doubt and caution to the techniques I was advocating, but after discovering how quickly John responded positively to them during home visits, she was soon convinced. Finally, John was discharged – not only from the Druids Heath Centre, but also from the care of the local authority: he returned, to the great delight of all, to live with his family, at the family home.

Not all had suitable homes and families to which to return, of course, and other tasks during my time at the Centre included supporting young people in the care of professional foster parents working for the centre, and on one occasion supporting at some length a young man approaching his eighteenth birthday, as he struggled to come to terms with independent living. He had been in care for many years, and his family and relatives had no contact with him. He needed much support, reassurance and encouragement before he was able to manage independently.

The emphasis at the Druids Heath Centre was on a combination of professionalism and caring. Nevertheless, not every piece of work was successful. Andrew was a young man of about sixteen years old. He had been transferred to the ACU because of his difficult behaviour at one of the residential units. He had been responding well to the programme of work that had been agreed with his keyworker, and for several periods of about an hour was allowed out of the unit unaccompanied, for specific activities. It was planned that he would soon be transferred back to his unit.

One evening, I was co-ordinating or leading the team of social workers on duty. The evening meal was coming to an end, and Andrew asked me to let him out for his programmed time out of the unit. I opened the door for him, locking it behind him as usual. I briefly went into the office, recording the fact that he had left the unit, as specified in his programme. I returned to join the staff and the other young people, who were chatting at the table. I guess it was around a quarter of an hour later that there was a knock at the front door. Looking through the window, I could see two police officers standing outside. I quickly let them in, showing them into the office.

After they had established who I was, and that Andrew did indeed live there, they told me the news. After leaving the unit, Andrew had somehow got hold of some glue, had sniffed the fumes, and had become intoxicated. Walking along the pavement, he had somehow lost his footing, and had fallen sideways into the path of an oncoming car. He had been killed instantly. I phoned Steve Petts, the Principal Social Worker in charge of the unit. Then, while Steve phoned the Director of the Centre to inform him, and travelled to the unit to take charge, my colleagues and I had the unenviable task of breaking the news to the other young people. Subsequently, I was given the task of phoning at their homes colleagues not on duty, to let them know what had happened. That they were not only highly professional but also deeply caring is shown by the fact that several of these were in tears when they discovered that Andrew had died.

Soon after beginning work at the ACU, we sold our house in Nuneaton, and bought a rather larger house in Walsall, a couple of miles from the ACU. This meant finding a new Church, and we began to seek God's leading about this. Our sons were now four years and one year old. Both Maggie and I had experienced the unsettling effects of frequent moves during our own childhoods, and both of us were aware that, since my conversion, God had moved us around rather a lot! We also felt that the demands of my shift work at the Druids Heath Centre and bringing up our sons meant that we did not really have the resources to take much active part in ministry within a Church. We prayerfully asked God for a period of stability to bring up our children, and a Church at which we could simply belong, and be ministered to and spiritually fed.

For a short time, we attended the local parish Church, but it soon became clear to both of us that we should look a little further. At that time, several people talked to us about St Thomas' Church in nearby Aldridge, and, after we had attended several services there, both of us felt that this was where God was leading us to become members. The Church had many members able and qualified to preach and to take services, and there was really no need for yet another reader. For the next years ahead, God provided through St Thomas' Church exactly what we had asked for, and apart for a short time when we were leading a house group, and a few occasions when I was asked to preach when the Church was between ministers, we took no leadership role in the Church there, although we made many good friends.

Nevertheless, there were occasional small signs of God's continued presence and blessing. Jesus taught that God is not only concerned with the major events in our lives, and that no detail is too small for his caring attention – that even the hairs on our heads are numbered. As we slowly did the work on the new house to make it the way we wanted it, the money we had saved for the purpose was spent, little by little. Finally, almost all of it was gone, and we had finished most of the decorating and other small improvements we had planned. We had even planted the garden – mostly lawn when we moved in – with flowering shrubs, thanks to a free offer we had found, promoting some product or other.

Of all our plans for the house, only one thing remained. The back garden was around a hundred feet long, and for much of it there was no fencing between our garden and those next door on each side. We had planned to buy fencing, but the money had run out. We had found out about prices, and the fencing needed would have cost many hundreds of pounds. It looked as though that would just have to wait, which was a shame, because we had wanted to be able to allow the children to play safely in the garden. Then from somewhere came the idea that we should pray about it – even though that seemed a very petty thing to bring before God. Maggie and I stood together in the garden, our arms around each other's shoulders, we bowed our heads together, and I led us in prayer.

"Lord, we bring you the fencing we feel we need to go from there to there…" (I pointed to places on the border between our garden and those of our neighbours) "… and from there to there. Lord, we just leave the fencing to you. We don't have the money for it, but we know that you can provide, if that's right for us. So we just surrender to you, and ask you to do your will." I was feeling slightly foolish as we walked back into the house. Still, we had given the matter to God, and we spoke no more about it.

A couple of days later, I was in the garden, and my neighbour called me over. He asked me whether we wanted some fencing. The company he worked for was replacing some wooden staging in the warehouse, and had offered it to their employees, in exchange for merely paying the cost of using the company truck to take it home. Delivery of the staging cost us a little under twenty pounds. We had not mentioned the fencing we wanted to anyone. The staging was all that we needed, made from thick, well-seasoned timber far stronger than that usually used for fencing; it is still in place some twenty-three years later.

Some time after this, we visited some friends we knew from our time at Weddington Church. There we met again Dave Smith, the friend who had so often visited us during my time at college. A lot had happened in his life, since we had last met. His marriage had ended, after his wife had begun a relationship with another man. Dave, having left the family home, was lodging temporarily with friends, but was going to be homeless in a few weeks time. Recently, Dave had been taken, by a Christian friend, to a meeting at a Nuneaton church, where an evangelist had spoken at length about what it means to become a disciple of Christ, and at the end of his talk, the evangelist had invited any that wanted to give their lives to Christ, to invite Him into their lives, to come to the front of the hall and to pray with counsellors who were waiting there. Dave told us that he knew at that moment that this was what he wanted, and described how, a few minutes later, with great joy, he had prayed, giving his life to Christ.

It was clear that something fundamental had changed in Dave. Despite his apparently desperate situation, he had about him a sense of joy and peace that I had never seen in him before. As I listened to him, I felt the growing certainty that God intended to use His house – the one that Maggie and I were living in – to provide Dave with somewhere to live. Discovering that Maggie was feeling the same conviction, I invited Dave to come to live at our house. With some surprise and evident pleasure, he accepted the offer. So it was that, soon after that meeting, Dave took up residence in our spare room. It was clear that Dave was really determined to follow through the commitment he had made after hearing the evangelist, and over the months that followed, he and I would often talk well into the night: he had so many questions to ask about his new found faith, and about the Bible, which he read at length and with real enthusiasm. He joined the Church that Maggie and I went to, and participated very fully in the life of the Church, living with us at our home for many months before finally being allocated a council flat nearby. He found employment in the area, working in a well-paid job for a Christian charitable organisation, and continued to be a frequent and very welcome visitor to our home for several years, before finally moving away from the area.

I have already referred to the very high quality social work done by the Druids Heath Centre. It was a great joy to me to be part of this work, the human results of which proved to me again and again that it was possible for good social work to make a real difference. The Druids Heath Centre was seen by many as a real centre of excellence, and so, I felt, it was. The trouble was that providing such quality care required high ratios of staff to young people, and a high proportion of qualified staff. This meant that the Centre was expensive, and cuts in local authority funding at that time meant that many Social Services Departments began to develop their own cheaper facilities for caring for difficult, disturbed or delinquent adolescents. As the number of young people registered with the Centre slowly reduced, month-by-month, it became increasingly clear that its days were numbered. Colleagues began talking about the very real possibility of the Centre closing, and the redundancy that would result.

As you can imagine, the prospect of unemployment was an alarming one for me, particularly as Maggie and I had taken on a large mortgage when we had moved into our new home. I did my best to surrender the whole issue to God, though I remember that my prayers became increasingly anxious as the Centre showed more and more signs that it was becoming unviable. Still, for some months, as I regularly scanned the social work journals for vacancies, I did not feel any leading to apply for any of the posts advertised, and I did nothing.

Then one day I saw an advertised post, which said, "Specialist Fostering Social Worker – Teenagers in Trouble". As I read about the vacancy, at Walsall Social Services, I began to feel again the feeling that had once been so strange, but with which I was now becoming familiar, the certainty beyond logical understanding, that God had prepared the way for me. My experience of working with 'teenagers in trouble' meant that I was well qualified for the post, especially as some of this had specifically been work with Druids Heath Centre clients placed in specialist fostering placements. I applied for the job. I was asked to come for interview, and when I did I was the only candidate there. After the interview I was asked to wait, and it was without surprise but with hearty thanks to God that I heard the two interviewers offer me the job. I guess I also felt a small stab of guilt as I realised that I was about to become part of yet another local authority's efforts to develop their own cheaper alternative to the Druids Heath Centre.

A few years later, while I was working at Walsall Social Services, I heard, with real regret, that the Druids Heath Centre was closing, and that most of its employees were being made redundant.

Chapter 8

Walsall Social Services

After two and a half years working at the Druids Heath Centre, looking on local authority social workers as 'the customer', it was slightly strange to find that I had joined 'the other side'. The team I joined was the Fostering and Adoption team, based at Walsall Civic Centre. The team occupied an area in a huge open plan office, which was otherwise filled with the desks of various administrators and clerks. It seemed to me very unsuitable accommodation for a team routinely handling confidential information about clients, and about those who had applied to foster or to adopt a child.

Working for the Druids Heath Centre, with young people many of whom could behave in threatening or dangerous ways had always resulted in a close and mutually supportive staff group. Interpersonal difficulties had always been quickly confronted and resolved; such support had been essential for the health and safety of all workers! This had ill-prepared me for the very different atmosphere of a local authority social services team – particularly one that, because most of the time it was dealing with those who wanted to foster or adopt, as opposed to dealing with clients, was not seen as being 'in the front line', in the way that an area social work team might be.

I was entirely a stranger to the kind of games playing, talking behind backs and general personal undermining that was commonplace there. The 'Big Boss' was Brian. He was one of the two interviewers who had offered me the job, and he was consistently friendly and helpful. The team leader who reported to him, and a number of the other social workers in the team treated me with great reserve and caution, which I really did not quite know how to handle. I am not sure that I would have been able to survive in that team, were it not for Reg. Until I arrived, Reg had been the only male member of the team, but unlike me he had the experience and wisdom that comes from years working as a field social worker in 'the front line' – an area social work team. Brian decided that Reg should be my guide and mentor as I learned my new role, and for that I am profoundly grateful, not only because he taught well the skills I would need for this specialist role, but also because he supported and coached me in how to cope with the 'games playing' which seemed a consistent feature of the team.

During the previous years, under Brian's capable leadership, the team had recruited and briefly trained more and more foster parents. As a result, there were no longer any children under the age of about twelve in the Borough's children's homes, and several of these had been closed. A small number of teenagers had also been fostered successfully. The three remaining homes, however, were full – mostly filled with teenagers whose behaviour was almost as 'challenging' as those in the Druids Heath Centre. Many of these were occasionally described as 'unfosterable'. It was to address the fostering needs of this particular group that I had been recruited, so first I needed to become familiar with the systems for fostering.

A few weeks after I had begun this learning process, Brian told me that the Deputy Director, Barry, wanted to see me. When I asked, he said that he didn't know what it was about, but had simply been asked to pass the message on to me.

At the appointed date and time, I presented myself to the Deputy Director's secretary, and was shown into his office. Barry was there, as was Phil, the Assistant Director responsible for childcare. I knew that the development of fostering for teenagers was receiving considerable interest from the directorate, and was expecting some questions about how the work was progressing. However, that was not why I had been summoned.

Looking a little uncomfortable and very grave, Barry told me in his gentle Welsh accent that he had been contacted by someone calling himself Roland Swanick, who had identified himself as an investigative journalist, working for the BBC. The man had told Barry that I was presently being investigated, and that I had left McIntyre House 'under a cloud', because I had been responsible for abusing many of the young men who were resident there.

I felt shock and disbelief. The false accusation was to my ears so preposterous that I really did not know how to respond. Spluttering, I protested my innocence, and somewhat inarticulately invited them to contact the warden of the hostel, to interview past residents of the hostel, to carry out absolutely any investigation they could devise to satisfy themselves of my innocence. It was like a bad dream, and I remember at one point feeling my heart racing wildly.

I do not know exactly how they investigated that allegation, but I suspect that my spluttering outrage and incoherent protestations were being very carefully observed and evaluated by these two very experienced men. Some days later, I was summoned again to Barry's office, and told that neither the BBC nor any other news agency they could find had ever heard of Roland Swanwick. The matter was closed, and my name was cleared. I have sometimes wondered who it was that made the phone call to Barry, and to this day I cannot think of anyone I have known who would have wanted to do such a thing. No further allegations were ever made from that day to this. However, it certainly led me to be aware of the vulnerability of caring professionals of all kinds – and especially those involved in childcare – to malicious false allegations.

Over the months that followed, I became increasingly familiar with the processes and skills required for the assessment, training and support of foster parents. Whenever an application was received from an individual or couple prepared to consider fostering a teenager, I was given the task of carrying out that assessment. Some months after I had joined the team, Reg was promoted to a post outside it, and I inherited the task of supporting most of the foster parents on his caseload, many of whom fostered teenagers. Through the new emphasis on fostering teenagers, the number of adolescents in foster care slowly increased. One of the Borough's remaining three children's homes was closed.

However, there was, in the other two children's homes, a very significant number of teenagers who were simply not candidates for conventional fostering, because their behaviour was just too challenging or difficult. I remembered many of the teenagers at the Druids Heath Centre who were successfully placed in family placements, thanks to high quality professional levels of training for the foster parents, the provision of high levels of support, and the payment of professional levels of remuneration, thus allowing at least one of a couple to have no other employment.

Even the best of children's homes is an unnatural environment compared with a family, and I began to argue that a professional fostering project, similar to that run by the Druids Heath Centre, could be run within Walsall Social Services. After all, a person only gets one childhood, and these young people in the children's homes were already emotionally damaged by their childhood experiences to date. Brian, and other social services managers, were sceptical. Innovative and creative fostering projects were all very well for Barnardo's, I was told, but could not possibly be successful in a local authority. I kept on arguing. Stubbornly, I pointed out that several other local authorities were already running such projects. Finally – I suspect because I was making a nuisance of myself – I was told to go and write a report about it, and authorised to use such time and travel expenses as that required.

It was not only informative, but also great fun visiting the professional fostering projects of local authorities and other social work agencies in the midlands. The social workers working in these projects often told stories of lengthy personal crusades to get them established and operating successfully. Many had an almost evangelical zeal about the work, which reflected my own, and were very happy indeed to share their experiences and advice. Thanks to their generous support and help, I was soon able to produce a lengthy paper, detailing the experiences of local authority Social Services Departments and other organisations who had already begun professional fostering projects for difficult adolescents.

Once the report was typed and given to Brian, it was difficult to go back to the routine of so-called 'mainline' fostering. My head was still filled with exciting ideas about a project to provide family life for the many young people in the children's homes who had absolutely no prospect of being placed in conventional foster families.

Reg, with a consideration and wisdom that was typical of him, suggested that, since the work I was doing entailed frequent contact with social workers in the area teams, I could usefully advance the cause by talking about the proposed project with many of them, and maybe even giving them copies of my report, so that if/when it happened, the idea of referring their adolescent clients to the project was not entirely new to them. I guess that chatting, and the canvassing of opinion among grass roots social workers probably helped the subsequent establishment of the project – but I suspect that the main reason Reg made the suggestion was because he could see my need to be doing something constructive towards it.

It was only a few weeks later, though it seemed like months, that Brian told me that the Director had read my report, and had approved the idea. A summary of my report was to form the basis of a director's report to the Social Services committee, recommending the establishing of a professional fostering project. I was very pleased – at last, after so many months of debating, arguing and persuading – some results!

Of course, it is one thing for the Director to recommend, quite another for the counsellors on the Social Service Committee to approve such a departure from the status quo. Happily, the Druids Heath Centre unwittingly helped to ensure the acceptability of the proposal, by choosing that moment to increase their already substantial fees. I heard that the increase was announced to the disgruntled counsellors of the Social Services Committee, together with the Director's advice that, at present, they had little choice other than to accept it, but that they would soon be asked to consider proposals that would reduce the dependence on the Druids Heath Centre.

The meeting of the Social Services Committee was a public meeting, of course, so any member of the public was entitled to attend (though not to speak), including social services employees. So on the night the report was to be presented to the committee, we filed in – Brian, a social worker called Mick who was to be seconded to the project from one of the children's homes, and me. The counsellors listened gravely to the Director's report, which bore a distinct resemblance to the paper I had written, but now said, "The Director has visited other local authorities... the Director found that..." and so on. With the latest Barnardo's price rises fresh in their minds, the counsellors asked the Director a few intelligent questions. Then they approved the new project, and the establishment of a new Team – the Adolescent Placement Team – to consist of a senior social worker, and three social workers, exactly as I had recommended, to recruit, train, and support professional foster parents to work in their own homes, caring for some of the most difficult teenagers in the Authority's care.

Afterwards, Brian made it clear that he had actually been in favour of the project all along. The sceptical attitude he had expressed so strongly was, he said, simply his way of ensuring that my arguments in favour of it were presented strongly in the paper, because he knew that others were sceptical about the idea. His portrayal of scepticism was certainly entirely convincing to me, and to this day it would be easy to have difficulty accepting that he was actually secretly supporting me all along.

Two of the three social worker posts and the senior social worker post were soon advertised. It was clear from the comments made to me by managers that they considered me a very strong candidate for the senior post, and I applied for this. I also applied for one of the social worker posts, just in case. In Walsall at that time, the counsellors made all senior appointments directly, and I found that I was on a shortlist of two, to be interviewed by members of the social services committee. To my surprise and dismay, the other candidate was appointed. I remember feeling more than a little hard done by, particularly as I had literally written the manual that was to be the basis of the project, and, while the person appointed had a background in social work with difficult adolescents in care, she had no experience at all of fostering.

Some days later, my sense of injustice was increased, when I was told that they had just realised, reading her application more thoroughly, that she had no driving licence. Since this was a basic requirement for the post, I was told, if they had noticed this lack earlier, she would not have been short-listed. I was later appointed to one of the social worker posts in the project.

At the time, I found all of this difficult to accept, and it was only after some stern talking to myself that I settled down and resolved to give my best to the work of developing the new project, particularly as the newly appointed Senior Social Worker's personal attributes and lack of fostering experience meant that she often needed considerable advice and support from me to fulfil her role. I do not remember whether that stern talking to myself included re-reading God's promise in the Bible:

"And we know that in *all things* God works for the good of those who love Him, who have been called according to His purpose". (Romans 8: 28)

At the risk of telling the story out of chronological order, I should say at this point that, in retrospect, it is easy to realise that **not being appointed** to the senior post was an extraordinary blessing. If I had been appointed to that senior post, I would probably still be working there. Like all local government officers, social workers are not allowed to engage in any other gainful employment or self-employment without the express approval of the local authority – i.e. the counsellors. That permission is rarely if ever given. Thus, had I been appointed to the senior social worker post, I would not have had the opportunity to develop, initially on a very part-time basis, the hypnotherapy, counselling and psychotherapy practice that became my full time living, and one of the great joys of my life.

While all this was going on, there was progress on another front. At Coventry I had studied with particular enthusiasm those subjects that were directly about helping clients with emotional and psychological difficulties. Especially interesting to me had been the substantial information and skills training to which the course had given me access. At the Druid's Heath Centre, my greatest pleasure in the work had been the opportunity to begin to put this learning into practice, supervised by capable and highly experienced senior staff.

The work at Walsall Social Services with foster parents and with young people in care had given me many more opportunities to develop these ways of working.

However, I was acutely aware that, while conventional counselling was sometimes very effective to enable an individual to change and move on as a result of new insights into themselves, on other occasions I would do my professional best, but the only result for the client would be new and deeper insights into why they were still as problem-ridden as ever.

Happily, my time at Coventry had also taught me how to research a subject properly, and I began an intensive search through the professional literature available. Finding an article that seemed to indicate a useful approach, I would locate and read textbooks cited by the authors. Two approaches seemed to stand out. The first of these was Hypnotherapy – a common enough word these days, in the 1980s it was scarcely heard of. I also came across another approach, occasionally vaguely referred to in the literature, often with comments about its 'magical' effectiveness, but never with any real description of its methods. The approach was called NLP.

NLP (short for Neuro-Linguistic Programming) is also an increasingly well-known field of study today, with important applications in management, business, education, coaching and other areas. In the 1980s, the initial development work had hardly been completed, and search as I might I could find little useful detailed information. Knowing that Peter Brentnall, my colleague in APT, was studying psychotherapy (specifically an approach called Transactional Analysis, or TA) I asked him if he had heard of NLP. He responded enthusiastically to my question. His TA tutor had some training in the approach, he told me, and he, Peter, had actually had the opportunity to observe a piece of NLP work done by his tutor with a client, to address a phobia.

"It really does work like magic", he told me. One moment the client had been unable to even think about the phobic object without symptoms of panic. Then Peter's tutor has led her through a piece of NLP work using guided visualisation and other techniques. The work took less than an hour, at the end of which, not only was the client able to talk about and visualise the phobic object without ill effects, she was apparently unable to reproduce the phobia symptoms even when challenged to do so! Peter had the opportunity to follow up that case, and many months later the client was still entirely free of the phobia that had blighted her life for many years. He recommended a book: "Frogs into Princes", by Dr. Richard Bandler and Dr. John Grinder, as a useful introduction to the subject.

As the reader will understand, I could hardly wait to get my hands on that book. I phoned a nearby bookshop and ordered it that same day. When it arrived, I waited impatiently for the weekend, when I would have the time to read it. The book was written as though it was a transcript of a teaching seminar, including demonstrations of work with the real live problems of those attending the seminar. (Later I found out that it had actually been composed from a number of videos of teaching seminars taught by Bandler and Grinder in America). After reading through the first couple of chapters, I found myself becoming increasingly excited by what I was discovering. Long before the end of the weekend I had finished the book, and had decided to order several others, mentioned in 'Frogs into Princes'. This was an approach that absolutely demanded further investigation!

During this time, I was also researching the field of hypnotherapy, reading articles in the professional literature, and borrowing or buying textbooks on the subject, which I read and re-read with growing interest. I approached this subject with more caution, because I had heard that some Christian writers considered that hypnosis was harmful, or even demonic. And yet, however carefully

I read those textbooks, I was unable to understand what those Christian writers could possibly be objecting to. I decided to consult David Butterfield, the minister at St Thomas' Church where Maggie and I were members. David very frankly told me that he had no knowledge of hypnosis, and no knowledge of the Christian critics of it – but he would find out, he told me, and get back to me. Some weeks later, he handed to me a thick bundle of papers – copies of articles by a number of Christian authors, critical of hypnosis.

I read these prayerfully, and with great care. All were condemning something very different from the clinical hypnotherapy I had been reading about in the textbooks. I was entirely in agreement with these authors' horror at what they were describing, amateurish and sometimes damaging uses of hypnosis as entertainment, so-called stage hypnosis. The articles either assumed without explanation that arguments that applied to stage hypnosis also applied to hypnotherapy, or simply listed what amounted to dogmatic assertions, unsupported by scripture or by any but the flimsiest evidence or logic. It occurred to me while reading some of these that such arguments would undoubtedly have been failed by examiners had I turned in such sloppy work in an assignment at Coventry. After some further discussion with David, he told me that he felt it was appropriate for me to make my own judgement and decision.

Some weeks later, in one of the professional Social Work journals, a training course was advertised. This was an accelerated certification course in hypnosis, for qualified mental health professionals. I phoned the college running the course, and they confirmed what I had expected: my C.Q.S.W. meant that I was qualified for entry onto the course. This left a lot of soul searching to do, because the cost of the course was £800, a great deal of money at that time, in 1989. On top of that, there would be hotel bills, as the college was in Yorkshire. I thought and prayed about this, and discussed it with my wife. Since I had learned all I could possibly expect to simply by reading, this seemed the only way to find out more.

In the event I did the course, which was teaching a combination of modern clinical hypnotherapy and NLP. I found that hypnosis was nothing more than the relaxation exercises and stress management techniques I had learned at Coventry – taught and practiced with an intense attention to detail which represented a level of excellence I had not hitherto encountered. These included the progressive muscular relaxation techniques which Maggie had been taught by midwives when she was pregnant with our first child, and guided visualization techniques like those I had learned some years before at a Christian Counselling course I had attended years before at the suggestion of Guy Cornwall-Jones, the minister at St James Church. It was not new techniques or methods, but the precision of their combination and practice that made them considerably more effective than anything I had previously discovered.

To my great pleasure, the course also included a comprehensive introduction to NLP, including methods which anyone with training in counselling could easily integrate into their practice. These included ways to enable the worker to establish real rapport at a very deep level with the client, and ways of specifying the outcome the client was seeking which would tend to enable the client, comparatively effortlessly, to move towards that desired outcome. Some NLP change techniques were also included, to enable changes in thinking and perception that would accomplish the desired outcome.

There was, in those days, no central professional association for hypnotherapy: each training school had its own, with a membership consisting almost entirely of its own ex-students. At the end of the course, I decided to join the hypnotherapy association established by the college. I had vague thoughts of practicing as a therapist, and membership would give me a basis for this. Others at Social Services knew, of course, that I had taken the course, and some were curious to find out more.

Brian was very quick to impress on me that it was not appropriate to use hypnosis when working with Social Services clients. I explained that what I had learned was no more than developments of therapeutic techniques commonly taught on social work training courses, with a different name or label, and that such ways of working had been used within social work for years to enable clients to achieve change. Brian listened and seemed to understand. Then he asked me again for an assurance that I would not be using hypnosis with Social Services clients or foster carers.

I was puzzled, and asked which methods specifically, of all those I had used in the past, I should now refrain from using. Brian didn't know, and simply asked the same question again. I listed a dozen or so techniques, from counselling, behaviour therapy, cognitive therapy, and other approaches commonly used in social work. All these were fine, said Brian, and asked again for an assurance that I would not be using hypnosis with Social Services clients. I gave Brian the assurance he wanted, still puzzled as to the precise definition of it.

This was the first time I had met with the extreme caution, apparently born of superstition and ignorance, with which some respond to hypnosis. I have sometimes met with the same response since then. The use of psychological techniques to enable a person to achieve deep, stress-busting relaxation, and to achieve other changes they are wanting is apparently, to some people, entirely acceptable, as long such ways of working are called stress management, deep relaxation, guided visualisation, autogenics, relaxation training, cognitive therapy, or any one of a myriad of words, other than the word hypnosis. After the end of the meeting with Brian, I reviewed our conversation in detail, and concluded with some surprise that I had simply made a commitment not to use the word 'hypnosis' to describe what I was doing.

(Parenthetically it is worth commenting here that I consider the use of hypnosis as stage entertainment to be irresponsible and potentially dangerous, particularly because those using it may have minimal training, and are unlikely to have the background training in counselling and psychotherapy to enable them to deal professionally and caringly with complications that may arise. I am also prepared to accept that it might be possible for satanic groups to misuse hypnosis to harm others, or even as a vehicle for the demonic, though I have never encountered evidence of this. However, the superstition with which some otherwise rational people respond to hypnosis seems to me about as logical as banning scalpels because they might be used for human sacrifice.)

I remained at Walsall Social Services for another year or so after completing the hypnotherapy training. The professional fostering project, known as the 'Adolescent Placement Team', had become well established. One of the Social Workers who had worked at the Druids Heath Centre in the Family Placements Unit there had come to join us in Walsall Social Services, appointed to the third social worker post that had been created within the APT. I knew him to be a sound and professional worker, and welcomed him into the team with real pleasure. The project had grown to around twenty placement families, and further expansion was planned. I had been working with Walsall Social Services for around five years, and was beginning to feel that my days in the Department were numbered.

When I saw, in a social work journal, an advert inviting social workers to apply for probation officer vacancies in the West Midlands Probation Service, that familiar nudge from the Holy Spirit was the first sign that I was, indeed, on the move again. By one of those 'co-incidences' with which I had become increasingly familiar since my conversion, I had recently met socially someone employed within the probation service, and she willingly briefed me, and provided copies of recent relevant articles about current issues in probation, including several about recent and proposed developments in legislation affecting the Probation Service. I do not think I had ever been so very well prepared for an interview.

When I was interviewed by the panel, consisting of one Deputy Chief Probation Officer and two Assistant Chiefs, I had again the irrational sense of certainty that I would be successful, and that I was just following the plan that God had already prepared for me. In particular, they seemed surprised and impressed by my familiarity with proposed legislation that would affect the Service, information with which I had 'coincidentally' been provided. At the end of the Interview I was asked to wait, and around twenty minutes later was offered the post of Probation Officer. The next stage of the adventure had begun.

Chapter 9

West Bromwich Probation Office

Having been interviewed and offered in principle the post of Probation Officer, I met with the Assistant Chief Probation Officer for the borough of Sandwell, the area in which it was proposed that I would begin working. Dick Marsh was a friendly and straightforward man, whose frank and open manner I found refreshing, though I guessed that some might find him a little overpowering. He greeted me cordially, and proceeded to give me a well-informed potted history of Sandwell, and the people and operations of the Sandwell Division of the West Midlands Probation Service. I could not but be impressed by this impromptu chat, revealing as it did a detailed and deep knowledge of the people and the area, though I suspected that some parts of that chat had been repeated many times before.

A few days later, at Dick's suggestion, I arranged to meet with Bill Brookes, the Senior Probation Officer at the West Bromwich Probation Office, one of the offices within the Sandwell area. Bill had been managing the probation office at West Bromwich for many years, and I found him instantly likeable. He was a large, balding middle-aged man with a kindly, gentle manner, a slightly old fashioned courtesy, and probably the softest and deepest voice I had ever heard. After a long and detailed chat about the office and the work, he introduced me to some of the Probation Officers in the office, finally leaving me in the capable hands of Paul Rogoff. Dick Marsh had told me about Paul. He was a long standing West Bromwich Probation Officer, tall, with thin features, a refined manner, and light grey hair that looked seriously overdue for a haircut. Later, I was to discover that his hair always looked like that, even straight after a visit to the barber. Dick, knowing about my Christian belief, had described Paul to me as a man with a strong faith, and I suspect that he was one of the reasons for proposing that I should begin working in a post at West Bromwich. I left, at the end of that first visit to the office, feeling optimistic about the prospect of working there.

Some weeks later, I arrived for my first day's work at West Bromwich Probation Office. This was something of a culture shock: I was shown to my office, introduced to my secretary, and issued with a variety of equipment, including a pocket sized tape recorder to be used for dictating letters, case records and other material for typing. As I sat in my office, organising desk drawers and filing cabinets, I could not help comparing this in my mind with my first day at Walsall Social Services, when I had been shown my desk in one corner of the vast open plan office, introduced to the one typist who typed for all of us, and issued with two biros, with the warning that I would have to produce them when they ran out, in order to be issued with replacements! All in all, as I looked around the rather nice room that was now my office, I felt very pleased with the change.

New probation officers – either newly qualified, or entering the service from other social work agencies – were appointed as 'Unconfirmed Officers'. For the first year, they were given a protected caseload, which meant that they did not work with the most dangerous clients, and that the number of clients they worked with was strictly limited. As an unconfirmed officer, I was to have access to considerable support, including a weekly meeting with the Senior Probation Officer (called a 'supervision session'). Towards the end of the confirmation year, I would need to produce a portfolio of the work I had done, and on the basis of this, and the evaluation of Bill Brooks the Senior and Dick Marsh the Assistant Chief Probation Officer, I would hopefully be approved, and become a confirmed officer. The West Midlands Probation Service had taken this a step further, as a result of difficulties in the past, and established policy was that for the first month unconfirmed officers went through an induction period, and were not allowed to hold any cases at all.

As you may imagine, the move from a bare minimum of facilities and a very full caseload to comparative luxury and a month with no responsibilities was quite a change. The month went by soon enough, and I began working with my first cases. These were comparatively minor offenders such as car thieves, and those who had committed fairly minor assaults, and similar crimes. Much of the work was about supporting clients to address those problematic areas of their lives that had led them into offending in the first place, and over the next year I became very familiar with the legal systems within which we operated, with the norms of the Service, and with the world, the hopes and the aspirations of clients. At the end of the year, I fairly painlessly became a confirmed probation officer.

At that time, the Probation Service was defined as a social work agency, and its task was to 'advise, assist and befriend' those entrusted to its care.

Nowadays, the Probation Service is a law enforcement agency, its prime responsibility is public protection, and officers work within very prescriptive and restricting regulations indeed. Those it works with are no longer referred to as 'clients', but as 'cases' or as 'offenders'. I understand that since these 'tough changes' were introduced, re-offending levels among those on probation have ***increased dramatically***. I assume that this must be seen as a coincidence, because I understand that, as a result, further even tougher changes are planned.

Much of a probation officer's work, then as now, was fairly uneventful routine. A few cases stand out in my mind. In the accounts that follow, names and some details have been changed, to protect confidentiality.

One of the essential requirements before a probation officer can be of any help to a client, of course, is that officer and client have some contact with each other. To ensure this, one of the requirements of a Probation Order was that the client must report to the probation officer when instructed to do so. One of my clients was Bob, a man in his early twenties, with learning difficulties. For many weeks, I had not seen Bob, despite several letters I had sent, giving him reporting instructions. I had discussed the case with Bill Brookes, who had told me that I would probably have to return Bob to court for Breach of Probation, which would mean that he would receive further punishment, or even that his Probation Order might be revoked entirely, and he might be sent to prison as a result.

Despite his lengthy record of petty thefts, I liked Bob, and I asked several of my more experienced colleagues for advice. All of them told me that the family was well known to the Probation Service, and to the criminal justice system in general. Bob and his brothers had all been before the courts many times. Since Bob lived with his parents, I told a group of several colleagues, as we discussed this, that I intended to visit them, to elicit their help to ensure that Bob reported as required. The suggestion met with uproarious laughter. When the laughter died down, my colleagues advised me against such an approach. One, more outspoken than the rest, said with the air of one who knew about these things, "Bob's Mum will just tell you to piss off." I decided to give it a try anyway.

After the office had closed for the evening, I knocked on the door of the home of Bob's family. Almost immediately, I knew that, somehow, the way had been prepared for me. The door was opened by one of Bob's brothers, and when I asked if I could speak to his parents, I was cordially invited into the house. Sounds of general hilarity were coming from the front room, and as I followed my guide into the room, I could see Bob's father in the armchair, surrounded by all of his sons. It was the father's birthday, and each of his sons had bought him exactly the same present, a six-pack of his favourite lager. He was in fine, if rather incoherent spirits, and the empty cans around the chair showed that he had already begun appreciating his birthday presents. His sons were generously helping him with the task.

I was offered a seat next to the father, and explained what I had come for. Bob's father listened to what I had to say, and then waving his beer can unsteadily, told me that I just didn't understand. Bob had gone to a 'backad' school. After a moment of puzzlement, I understood that he meant the word 'backward'. He had always been 'backad'. The rest of us really couldn't expect him to remember appointments, because he was 'backad', and just couldn't do it. I nodded sympathetically. It must be terrible for him, I said. The father agreed gravely that it was.

With my best sympathetic voice, and a straight face, I asked how often this terrible affliction meant that Bob had lost benefit payments because he had forgotten to sign on as unemployed. Father stared at me silently, looking more and more confused, as I waited politely for his reply. Suddenly, he threw his head back, laughing loudly with real amusement, before turning to Bob: "I've done me best for yer son! – But yer've got no chance with this one – 'ee knows!" The whole family was laughing now, and suddenly, I seemed to be everybody's best friend. It was with some difficulty that I managed to decline the open can of beer that someone stuffed into my hand. I left the house half an hour later, with everyone's assurances that I was 'alright', and that I was 'safe'. (In the slang, that meant that they felt safe with me). From that day until the end of the order, Bob kept every appointment with me, and even seemed a little disappointed when the probation order came to an end.

Mike was another client of mine. He was different from many in that he was in full time work – he had worked on building sites for many years. He was also as honest as the day is long. His problem was that, again and again, when he went out with colleagues for a drink after work (well, quite a few drinks, actually) he would end up fighting. He had a string of convictions for assault and affray as a result. In many ways he was difficult to work with, because the man who regularly kept his appointments with me in my office was genuinely remorseful for his behaviour, and totally determined to avoid any further violent offending – till the next time he 'had a few drinks' with his mates, and ended up in yet another drunken brawl. To make matters worse, he had won the reputation as 'the hardest man in West Bromwich', and felt a certain pride in this. After many deep and earnest conversations had been entirely ineffective, I made a new plan for working with him, and saved it for the time when another violent offence brought him again before the court. I did not have long to wait.

Then, as Mike went into his usually pattern of remorse, I suggested that he was not being sincere. He began to earnestly assure me with real intensity that his regret was real, and that he would do anything to get away from the pattern of repeated violent offending. "Anything?" I asked. **"Anything!!!"** he replied emphatically. So I suggested that he should join a local full-contact Karate club, "if he had the bottle". (Most Karate styles teach participants to pull their punches and other blows, to avoid injuring each other when they practice – full contact Karate clubs are comparatively few and far between – they pull no punches).

Some weeks later Mike was reporting to me again. He had put off the agreed task for some days, but had finally borrowed a 'judo suit' and gone along to the club. He told me about his first evening. After the leader of the club had welcomed him and introduced him to the other members, he asked Mike about his experience of martial arts. Mike said that he had none, but explained that he was a very accomplished street fighter. The club leader smiled, and suggested that Mike could show what he could do in a contest with one of the club members. He pointed out a short, skinny man. Mike told the club leader that if he fought the little chap with all his might, he could well do him serious injury, and suggested that another, larger member be chosen for the contest. The Instructor insisted that Mike fight the little man. Three times Mike tried to attack the diminutive chap, and somehow none of his blows met their target. Three times, when his opponent's blows landed, Mike was on his back again, with yet more bruises. Mike was seriously impressed.

Many months later, for the first time in years, Mike's Probation Order was about to come to an end, and he had committed no further offences. So for the first time in some years Mike was about to be free of the need to report to a probation officer. He was reporting to me for the last time. He was now a respected member of the club, having risen rather rapidly through the ranks, due to his exceptional ability to learn. He was now teetotal, because he was determined to maintain his high level of fitness, as befits a dedicated athlete. He told me about a recent encounter with violence at a local pub. Mike and several other club members were sitting at a table in the pub, with their non-alcoholic drinks. A customer who had obviously had rather too much to drink was becoming increasingly obnoxious, and trying to pick a fight. Mike walked over to him, and quietly told him that he was advising him to leave. **Now.** The man looked at Mike, and recognised something of Mike's confident manner as he said this. He decided to accept Mike's advice and he left the pub. Mike told me that he had realised with horror that he himself had been just like that man less than a year earlier.

Sometimes, unfashionable as it was in those days, it was necessary to take a more authoritarian approach. Ross was a man in his early twenties, who had always treated me, his latest but certainly not his first probation officer, with polite reserve, cautiously holding me at arms length. I was aware that when he reported he was holding back a great deal, and I guessed that he was similarly cautious with other authority figures. Like many young offenders, the parenting he had received had been poor. He had a growing record of convictions for offences of theft. Like many such young men, he claimed to have great difficulty organizing himself and his life. Ross had failed to report several times, and there was a real danger that he would face proceedings for breach of probation if this were to be repeated.

One day, he failed to report again, despite having agreed the date and time of his appointment at the previous meeting. I drove to the flat where he lived with his mother, and knocked on the door. His mother answered the door, and told me that Ross was not there: he had gone to the local shops. At the shops, I spotted a group of young men including Ross, standing and talking. Simulating an anger I did not feel, I marched toward the group, roundly rebuking Ross in front of his 'mates', and pointing out that he could now expect to be taken back to court for failing to report. Then I imperiously ordered him to get into my car. We drove in silence to the Probation Office, then at my terse instruction, he followed me up the stairs and into my office, waiting for my instruction to do so before sitting down. I told him brusquely that, as he had now reported as instructed, I would not need to summons him to court.

Ross was looking at me in a new and very different way I can only describe as loving. His manner was completely different from the slightly clueless, disorganised young man I had always encountered before. It was clear that my actions, in coming out to get him rather than just 'doing my job' and returning him to court, had somehow touched him in a new way. From then until the end of the Probation Order almost a year later, he invariably reported to me whenever instructed to do so. He was now prepared to share openly about himself, and to put into practice the changes we discussed. It was almost as though the combination of strictness and caring were fulfilling a need that had been left unsatisfied, and he treated me like a loved and respected father. Over ten years after Ross' Probation

Order came to an end, shortly before I left the Probation Service, I checked the name on the computer system. He had never been in trouble again.

As well as working with specifically allocated clients, as a probation officer I had other duties. Among these was taking my turn on the rota as Duty Probation Officer. Some of those who called at the office seeking some service were people who were not allocated to a particular officer, (there was a pool of unallocated cases) or whose probation officer was not available at the time. Others who called at the office were not on probation at all, or lived in some other part of the country. The Duty Officer was responsible for seeing these. This could include clients, for example, presenting with a crisis, such as suddenly becoming homeless, and needing help to locate somewhere to sleep that night. In a day on office duty, anything could happen – or nothing could happen at all.

There were a number of alcoholic men living in the area, many of whom reminded me of men we had met at Cambridge Cyrenians. For the most part, they were unkempt in appearance, with an approach that alternated between mild verbal aggression and extreme pathos, and they had about them the characteristic musty smell of the chronic alcoholic. Many of these were not on probation, and had no official link with the service, but that didn't stop them calling at the office at regular intervals. At that time, part of the budget for each office was a 'befriending fund' as it was called. If a client was in financial difficulty, a probation officer could sign to authorise a payment of up to £5. The Senior Probation Officer could authorise up to £10. The local alcoholics knew this well, and would call at the office asking for financial help for any number of reasons, mostly fictitious. Sometimes they were successful in persuading a duty officer to authorise a payment, and the reality was usually that the money would soon be spent on alcohol.

I very soon decided that it would be a mistake to yield to the temptation to simply give a payment when asked, although this was certainly the short term easy answer. I remember on several occasions spending over half an hour refusing a payment in spite of his arguments to well-known local drinker who would happily have left within two minutes if I had meekly given the requested £5 befriending fund grant. Soon, my reputation spread among the local drinkers. When a receptionist phoned my office to tell me that someone unknown to the service needed to see the Duty Officer, I usually replied by saying that I would be there in ten minutes. Usually, when I walked into the waiting room after only five minutes, there would be no one there. Often, the man would ask the receptionist who was on duty, and hearing that it was Dave Carpenter would say something uncomplimentary about wasting his time and would leave.

It was in the nature of the job that an apparently monotonous and routine day could suddenly change completely. One day, I was on office duty, and the phone in my office rang. The receptionist said that someone not known to us wanted to see the duty officer. I asked her to tell the caller that I would be able to see him in ten minutes. The receptionist paused, then said, "Dave, would you see this one now? He's really worrying us." I said I would come straight away. This was a very experienced receptionist: if she was worried, it would be with good reason. I walked into the client waiting room to find a tall, unshaven man pacing the floor angrily in the otherwise empty room. I smiled, extended my hand to shake hands, told him my name and asked how I could help. He ignored my offered hand, and held his outstretched right forefinger an inch from my nose, shouting a string of obscenities. Moving slowly and speaking quietly, I sat on a bench seat in the room, inviting him to take a seat. The receptionist had been right: his manner and movements were those of one accustomed to violent solutions to almost any problem. Once seated, he began again shouting and using obscenities in a way that I guessed had successfully intimidated many in the past. I mildly pointed out that he hadn't heard me swear at him, and asked him not to swear at me.

He began again, only slightly less aggressively. He was a traveller, he told me, living in a caravan. His van was in London, and he was stranded here with no money. He demanded £35 so that he could take the train back to London. When I asked, he confirmed that he was not on probation, and did not have a probation officer. I explained politely that I was only able to give grants to probation clients, and even then the maximum I could authorise was £5. It was as though he had not heard me at all. He repeated his story. I repeated my response. He repeated his story again, demanding £35. I repeated my reply gently, as I stood up and walked over to the outside door. Repeating that I was sorry that there was nothing I could do to help, I opened the door, and politely stood back to allow him to leave.

His face suffused with anger, he walked quickly towards me, watched from behind their window by the reception staff. He stopped when his face was only four or five inches away from mine. I recognised the move. He was lining up to head butt me. By moving his head forward and downwards quickly, he could strike my face with his forehead, breaking my nose at least. I considered taking off my glasses, and decided not to. With his rancid breath in my nostrils, and seeing his staring eyes mere inches from mine, I heard his voice, low and menacing. "So what are you saying?" he grated.

I fought to quell rising fear and to keep my voice calm and mild as I replied. "What I'm saying is that I've treated you with unfailing courtesy and respect, so I know you're going to treat me the same way, aren't you?" For what seemed like a very long time, we stood immobile, he scowling into my face while I waited politely for his reply, trying to look as inoffensive as possible. Then suddenly, he turned his back on me, and without a word walked out of the open door. After a moment, I moved to shut the door behind him, and saw him walking on the short path that led from the probation office to the road. He was walking slowly, shaking his head as if in puzzlement. I closed the door, and heard the concerned question of the receptionist – was I all right? It was half an hour before I stopped shaking.

During my induction month, Bill Brookes had made a point of putting aside time to chat generally, apart form 'official' supervision sessions, and inevitably my interest in psychotherapy had come up for discussion. Bill encouraged me to use the resources of the library at Probation Headquarters in Birmingham, particularly to research applications to the work of the probation service. This was the first time since I had been at Coventry that I had been given access to a good academic library, and I decided to make the most of it. I soon found a number of articles in the professional literature about the use of NLP in social work, and in the work of the Probation Service.

In particular, I found one very insightful article by a Probation Officer whose name I have no record of now – I believe it was Bob Anderson. When I told Bill that Bob was working as a Probation Office in the next county, he encouraged me to arrange to meet him. When I met Bob Anderson, I discovered that he had actually completed a period of full time study and research – a 'personal research fellowship' at the nearby university, at the end of which he had produced a lengthy paper, "The Application of Neuro-Linguistic Programming to the work of the Probation Service". I took back with me from that meeting a copy of his paper, and used copies of it in my attempts to elicit some enthusiasm for NLP in the West Midlands Probation Service. However, that was not to be.

Nevertheless, the visit to Bob Anderson renewed my enthusiasm for NLP, and during the two and a half years I was at the West Bromwich Office, I first completed Foundation Skills Certification, then Certified NLP Practitioner training, and thanks to Bill Brookes' support and advocacy, the Probation Service gave me study leave to complete the various modules of the courses, varying in length from three days to almost two weeks.

Nowadays, good quality NLP training is available throughout the country. In those days in the 1990s, however, London was almost the only place in the UK where quality NLP training was to be found. This made the training not only inconvenient but also expensive, requiring much staying in hotels, and much driving up and down the motorways. This, and the training itself were hard work, but this was more than compensated for by the recurring sense of wonder and delight at the things I was learning, and the growing conviction that this was part of the path that God intended for me. I do remember my motivation being severely tested on several occasions by a three hour drive to London at the end of a day's work for a two hour skills practice group (part of NLP Practitioner training) followed by a three hour drive back up the motorway to the Midlands...

The examination at the end of the Practitioner course was rigorous, and entirely based on the demonstration of skills, rather than mere knowledge. To my great disappointment, I discovered on the last day that I had not yet achieved the required standard, and that my certification as an NLP Practitioner was to be deferred, until I had successfully completed further work. A Master Practitioner, one of those who had been assisting the trainers on the course, was appointed as my mentor, and I knew that I would have to satisfy him that I had the appropriate level of competence before I would be granted the coveted NLP Practitioner Certificate. I notice that the Practitioner Certificate that now hangs framed on the wall in my consulting room is dated 1st October 1991, the date on which the course ended. It was not until March of the following year that I reached the necessary standard to be awarded it, and towards the end of March 1992 when I received the certificate through the post, I took it out of its envelope with a great feeling of satisfaction and achievement.

A comment is appropriate here. I have since experienced the training of many world class NLP trainers at first hand, including that of Dr. Richard Bandler and Dr. John Grinder, the two eminent researchers whose brilliant research originally brought the field of NLP into being, and many others who are internationally known authors of standard NLP textbooks. I consider that the Practitioner training I received from Pace Personal Development (PPD) is the finest and most sensitive training I have ever experienced. Let me warmly recommend PPD to any reader who is considering training in NLP, and wondering with which of the many NLP training organisations in the UK to train.

Soon after completing the Hypnotherapy Training course, I began to see a small number of private clients for hypnotherapy, counselling and NLP therapy at our family home. I had placed occasional advertisements in local newspapers, and some of those who responded to these found the work sufficiently useful that they told others, who subsequently contacted me. This meant that one or two evenings each week were usually spent seeing clients at home. Maggie and our two sons were very understanding and tolerant of this 'hobby' activity as they saw it, and all got used to sitting very quietly in the lounge while 'Dad has a client'. This little hobby seemed a small thing at the time, but was to grow to become my full time living.

During this time, there was an important development in the field of counselling and psychotherapy, which was to have a major effect. Some years before, the British Association for Counselling (now the

British Association for Counselling and Psychotherapy) had called a conference of the many different organisations that represented the many different approaches to psychotherapy. That conference, the UK Standing Conference on Psychotherapy (UKSCP) had continued to meet from that time. Although NLP was originally born out of research into psychotherapy, it has many applications, including business, education, management, coaching, and others. In order to represent the needs specifically of those using NLP therapeutically, a separate section of the Association for NLP was formed. Called the Psychotherapy And Counselling Section, it was usually referred to as the ANLP PCS. It was one of the organisations that sent delegates to the Standing Conference for Psychotherapy.

Subsequently, the UK Standing Conference for Psychotherapy became the UK Council for Psychotherapy (UKCP). Its member organisations were asked to provide a list of their accredited psychotherapists, for inclusion in the first UKCP Register of Psychotherapists. It was clear to me and to many others that this was going to become an increasingly important way for the public to identify properly trained psychotherapists. The ANLP PCS, after much deliberation, decided that the NLP training standard required for accreditation as an NLP psychotherapist would be Master Practitioner Certification. In order to be eligible for this, I would need to take further NLP training.

I felt a great sense of urgency. I was well aware that, once the UKCP Register was established, the requirements for registration could be expected to become steadily more demanding over the years. It was going to be far easier if I were able to get onto the register at an early stage. It seemed to me so clear that I had to act quickly that I made a major mistake. I just got on with the urgent business of choosing an organisation with which to train. Specifically, I did not consult God in prayer – either about whether to train at this time, or about which organisation to train with.

Actually, in failing to consult with God, I was taking to myself the control of that part of my life. As that part of my life ceased to be under His lordship, it also ceased to be under His protection. I learned an important lesson through this. In the event, I was to pay dearly for my error. It seemed to me obvious that I should take Master Practitioner training as soon as possible, and I simply chose the NLP training organisation whose training timetable would allow me to qualify at the earliest possible date.

A central part of the training course I chose was a residential module. In order to cram in all the training required, training was all day, and all evening too. I had agreed with Maggie that she would have the car for that time, and I would travel to the course by motorbike, to the venue in the countryside, well over a hundred miles from our home. I had always enjoyed motorcycling, and the journey, deep into the countryside, was a real pleasure. Arriving at the venue, I was directed to the room that was to be my home for the time, and unpacked my bags. The training began later that day.

Over the days that followed, we trainees – about thirty of us – worked very hard indeed. The very complex material we were learning was conveyed in a succession of lectures or presentations interspersed with exercises to integrate and practice the skills we were learning. The days began to blend into each other, and it was hard to keep track of all that we were being taught. We would begin training after breakfast, and apart from short breaks for meals would often continue working and training until after ten at night. Often there would be further homework tasks to complete after that as well. Of course, after working so intensively, most of us needed to unwind before we could sleep, and we would gather in the bar for a drink before retiring for the night.

As the days went by, I became increasingly short of sleep. One result of this was that I found it increasingly difficult to understand the material we were being taught. I became increasingly confused, functioning less and less well, while all the time trying to keep up with the course and to apply myself conscientiously to the work. As the final day of the residential module came closer, I realised that I was seriously unwell. I was certainly not in any fit state to return to work. In fact, I am quite sure that I could not safely have ridden the motorcycle home.

Several others seemed to be similarly affected. Others of my fellow trainees seemed to be changing personality in a way that seemed almost sinister – people who had been pleasant and friendly at the start of the course were becoming progressively stranger in their behaviour: sometimes they were distant, at others they were behaving as though there was a secret 'in joke' – responding with barely concealed amusement to the difficulties others were experiencing.

On the last day, feeling very unwell indeed, I telephoned Maggie. She drove through the night, with our two sons in the back of the car, and it was with a great feeling of relief that I heard the familiar sound of the diesel engine of our car through the open window of my room. I do not think I had slept at all for several days. My thinking was confused, and I was often not able to remember events of even a few minutes ago. I found all of this very frightening indeed. Maggie drove us home.

When I saw our family doctor the next day, he had no hesitation in signing me off sick for a month. I had lost well over half a stone in the two weeks, although my recollection is that I was eating well throughout. For several days after returning home, I desperately needed sleep, but my constantly racing thoughts made that impossible. At the next module of the course some weeks later,

I discovered that I was not the only one to experience adverse effects, at the end of the intensive module. Several others told me they had taken weeks to recover. One lady, whose Multiple Sclerosis had been in remission for years, was now very ill, hardly able to walk, and had attended this shorter module only because of her determination not to give in to it. Of course multiple sclerosis is a disease that can go into spontaneous remission for long periods and then reoccur, so maybe it was just coincidence.

At the end of that final module of the course, we were given final tasks to complete. Once these were completed successfully and returned, we would be awarded our certification as Master Practitioners of NLP. During the next few days, I found myself questioning deeply the quality and nature of the training we had received. Happily, I had the very good experience of training with Pace Personal Development (PPD) with which to compare it.

During Practitioner training with PPD for a group of around twenty trainees there had always been, in addition to the trainer, at least two or three assistants, all Master Practitioners, to help individuals with exercises, and to generally assist with difficulties. Sometimes training raised painful issues from a person's past, for example, and an assistant was always on hand to work with a person as needed, to resolve such problems. During the master practitioner training with this second company, for a group of around thirty, there was just one assistant to assist trainees. A second assistant was assisting the trainers rather than the trainees; he was there, he said, because he was training as an NLP trainer. He was learning from the trainers, and I did not at any time see him assisting trainees with difficulties.

Also, comparing the two courses, I realised that there was something not quite right about the Master Practitioner course. During the practitioner course with PPD, I remember feeling that trainers and assistants were not only very capable but also very caring in the way that they dealt with us all. Looking back on the Master Practitioner course, it seemed to me that some of those involved with the course were the sort of people, frankly, from whom one might hesitate to buy a used car. I realised that the lack of real caring or trustworthiness had actually been evident from the beginning, and I wondered that I had overlooked or ignored it. It occurred to me that, if I were practicing as a therapist with that training organisation's certificate on the wall of my consulting room, it would imply that I was endorsing their training. I began to wonder if I could morally justify this.

As I continued to be off work on sick leave, I prayed about all of this, sometimes alone, sometimes with Maggie, sometimes with other Christians, members of St Thomas' Church. One married couple there – longstanding friends of ours – when we prayed together at the end of a time together, prayed for my healing. The husband, a quiet and modest man, not given to sensationalism, prayed that any attack on me that was demonic in nature should cease. He laid his hands on my shoulders as he prayed. The relief I felt was palpable and immediate. It was as though a great load had been taken from my shoulders. Just as suddenly, I knew that I would not be asking for certification from that training company. I also knew that I would very soon be back at work. A few days later, as the sickness certificate was about to run out, I visited the doctor again. It was clear both to him and to me that my recovery was complete, and that I was fit again. He signed me off as fit to return to work.

I soon returned to the old routine at West Bromwich Probation Office, and soon I was absorbed again in the work with clients. I continued to see private clients at my home, and found this to be a refreshing balance: not every probation client was necessarily happy to be attending the appointment, or committed to engaging fully in work to enable him to make major changes! It was a great source of pleasure to me, therefore, to be working in the evenings with clients who were very committed to working towards the solutions to the problems that had brought them to me. Indeed, these private clients were not only appreciative of effective quality work; they absolutely expected and demanded it – after all, they were paying for it! I felt that working with clients who were also customers, and who, at the end of each session, were making a positive decision to book and to pay for their next appointment (or not!) was both refreshing and a constant motivation for me to maintain the highest quality of which I was capable.

Among the many members of the caring professions I met during the time at West Bromwich was Nigel. He was a manager of an addiction clinic in West Bromwich. He and I soon found that we got on well, and that we had much in common, including the fact that Nigel had also trained in hypnotherapy. We had a number of clients in common too, which gave us good reasons to meet regularly. He was to play a small but important part in the future growth of the private practice.

Another important contact was also made at this time. Shortly before NLP Practitioner training I began attending an NLP practice group in Birmingham. (There are groups of this kind all over the country to enable those with an interest and/or training in NLP to meet together to practice their skills). One member of that group was James Middleton. There was a good deal that I wanted to ask James, because he was a practicing hypnotherapist, working at home. We soon found that we had a lot in common, and I was impressed both by his gentle nature and by his creative thinking. We soon became firm friends, and at the time of writing that firm friendship had continued for some sixteen years. I had no way of knowing that he too was to play a small but essential part in the establishing of the private practice.

Chapter 10

More Moves

The Prophecy

At that time, it was the policy of the West Midlands Probation Service that no Probation Officer should spend more than a certain amount of time in one post. I cannot remember the time limit – it has changed since then. By the time I had been at the West Bromwich probation office for around two and a half years, all of the officers who had been there when I arrived had left, including Bill Brookes the Senior Probation Officer, who had been moved or directed to another post. Although my recollection is that I had another couple of years before having to worry about a move to another post against my will, I decided that it was time to start looking around: frankly, I wanted some control over where I went, so I decided to jump before I was pushed!

One of the Probation Hostels run by the Service was advertising for a Deputy Manager. Having worked in a probation hostel for five years as an Assistant Warden, I wondered whether this might be the right post for me. In large organisations, the internal gossip can be inaccurate or downright wrong, but as I asked around about the vacancy, I heard that the last Deputy Manager at that Hostel had experienced a major nervous breakdown, and was still off sick and unable to work two years later.

I decided to proceed with caution. I visited the Manager of the hostel by arrangement. She was a middle aged woman, rather older than I, with many years of experience, and as I chatted with her about the work, and the way the hostel was run I could find nothing to suggest that there were any major problems of the kind that might be the cause of such an affliction. As we chatted, I wondered whether to bring the matter up. Before I had reached a decision about that, the Manager herself did so. She talked about the illness her previous Deputy had suffered, and emphatically told me that, if I were appointed, she would absolutely insist that I inform her fully about any difficulty I experienced with her management style. I was happy to give her the assurance she was seeking.

I also met with several of the Assistant Wardens working there, and the team seemed a genial and happy one. I decided to apply for the post, and soon after was interviewed by the Assistant Chief Probation Officer responsible for residential services. It did occur to me to wonder when I realised that I was the only person being interviewed, particularly as I had heard a rumour that I was the only person who had applied. Still, I was pleased when I was offered the post. I began to work at the hostel a few weeks later.

The job I had been doing for the last two and a half years as a field Probation Officer had involved a considerable amount of time working with paper rather than with people, and I was looking forward to spending rather more of my time working directly with probation clients, now that I was working in a hostel again. Hostel work had a reputation for being stressful, but I had already survived for five years at McIntyre House, and the prospect of a return to hostel work held no great fears for me.

During the weeks that followed, everything seemed to go smoothly, and I enjoyed the far closer working relationships of the residential setting. The role of Deputy Manager was a mixture of supervisory/management tasks and professional/legal tasks, as I was also probation officer to the residents there. It involved rather less contact with the day to day running of the hostel, as there were

Assistant Wardens to do most of these tasks, and domestic staff to do much of the cleaning, cooking, and household management. Tasks of the Assistant Wardens included much of the direct individual work with residents. On arrival, a new resident would be assigned a 'Keyworker' from among the Assistant Wardens, who was then responsible for working with that resident, under the supervision of either the Manager or me.

All residents were living at the Hostel on the basis of a legal requirement to do so. Some were subject to a Probation Order with a condition of residence at the hostel. Others, convicted of an offence but yet to be sentenced, were required to live there as a condition of bail. Yet others, having served a prison sentence for an offence, were required to live at the hostel as a condition of their parole. Sometimes a resident would disappear, usually taking all his belongings with him, so one of the professional tasks that fell to me as the Probation Officer was, as an officer of the Court, to formally attend the court, giving the details of events under oath, and to apply for a warrant for the arrest of the absconder. There were some officers who enjoyed the work in court very much, and even some who chose to specialise in it. I must say that it was my least favourite parts of the work, particularly because, as a hostel deputy manager, if I was attending court it meant that the work with that particular client had been unsuccessful.

For many years, there has been an established practice in social work, called the supervision session. This is a period of time (usually an hour) set aside for a worker to spend with his/her immediate line manager, discussing his/her progress, professional needs, any problems, personal development, and so on. While the word 'supervision' makes it sound like an imposition, it is actually a time when the agenda is entirely about the professional, training, and development needs and the work of the person being supervised, and most people will look forward to their monthly supervision session. My role as Deputy Manager included acting as supervisor to around half of the Assistant Wardens, a role I took on with great pleasure.

When I had been Assistant Warden at McIntyre House, the work had included sleeping at the hostel when on the rota to do so, called 'sleeping in duty'. Another great pleasure was that, as Deputy Manager, I was not required to do this. However, merely working from nine to five would have meant very little meaningful contact with residents, and I began the habit of spending the occasional evening at the hostel. Once the Assistant Wardens realised that I was not checking up on them, and that I still expected them to run the hostel exactly as though I was not there, they seemed entirely happy with this. I spend many hours getting to know residents better over the pool table, or just chatting informally in the television room, and this became a part of the job to which I actively looked forward.

It seemed that I had found, at the hostel, a role to which I was ideally suited, but his idyllic situation was not to last. The nature of a probation hostel is that life there is a constant series of changes, as residents arrive and leave, and this tends to mean that life is a series of crises. The role of Deputy Manager was a new one to me, and of course that meant that I was relying heavily on the guidance of the hostel Manager, particularly as my five years of experience as an Assistant Warden had been at a juvenile hostel, not one for adults, and had ended around eight years before: residential practice, and the legal framework within which a probation hostel functioned, had changed considerably during that time. However, as the months went by, it seemed to me that I was being expected to know progressively more that I had never been told or taught.

Again and again, during this or that crisis, when I was 'the man on the spot', I would confidently make the decision that I considered to be appropriate and in accord with guidance or opinions the manager had expressed to me at other times. Again and again the manager would subsequently tell me that I had made the wrong decision, or handled the situation badly. I conscientiously applied myself to learning from this feedback. However, a diet of constant criticism, and instructions about what **not** to do, with little or no guidance about what to do in stead, and a complete lack of feedback to suggest that I was ever doing anything **right** had its inevitable result. I became increasingly stressed. It is a great blessing that this was at a time when I had no private clients. Finally, driving home from work one day, I found myself in tears, for no obvious reason. Recognising belatedly the symptoms of burnout, I went to the doctor the next day. He had no hesitation in certifying me as unfit for work, describing my ailment on the certificate as 'nervous debility'.

Feeling very stressed, I was also feeling very stupid. Here was I, a therapist who had been teaching the skills of stress management and stress recognition to others for years, failing to recognise the symptoms in myself. Of course, it was now obvious, and it was also obvious what I should do about it – see a therapist! I contacted my good friend and fellow-therapist James Middleton, and over the following days and weeks I visited him many times. Several conversations with another friend, a management consultant, and numerous lengthy sessions with James helped me to begin to make sense of my situation.

After much thought and discussion, I decided that I could best make complete sense of what had happened at the hostel if I treated the hostel as a case study in work stress, and wrote exactly as careful and professional an analysis as I would have written if it had been an assignment when I was a social work student at Coventry. Of course, making sense of the process was an important part of getting better: I had no wish to be off sick and unable to work for years, like my predecessor in the post. I researched conscientiously the assignment I had set myself, and that included many visits to the local reference library. Often they had to obtain from elsewhere the textbooks and research papers I needed to refer to. I remembered the undertaking I had given to the hostel Manager to give her information about any experience of difficulty with her management style, and after some thought, I decided to write the piece as a personal letter to her, so that she could decide whether to share the piece with others, or to keep it as a personal and private communication.

Having first handwritten the final draft, I dug out the old typewriter on which I had typed assignments as a student, and painstakingly typed out the piece, complete with bibliography; it came to 11 typewritten pages: not as long as a student assignment, but a substantial enough piece of academic work, and by the time it was completed, I felt a certain pride in a job well done. As I researched, wrote and then typed the piece, the process that had led to my illness became progressively clearer. It also became clear to me that, in order to protect myself from any reoccurrence in the future, I would need to be considerably less willing to accept without complaint the inconsistency, negativity and lack of clarity that were constant features of the management style under which I had been working.

So it was that, after many weeks of sick leave, I returned to work at the hostel. Within days of my return, I had a supervision session with the Manager. I presented to her the letter I had written. After a cursory glance at the first few pages, she put it away for later perusal, saying she would not read it now. Later she told me that she had given it to the Assistant Chief Probation Officer, so that it might form the basis of discussions during her supervision sessions with him.

I had now been in the post for around six months. I have mentioned already that probation policy set a maximum length of time an officer could spend in one post. The policy also set at two years the minimum time an officer needed to spend in a post before being allowed to move on to another. I had been back only a very short time before I realised that nothing was going to change in the near future, and that the factors that had led to my illness, carefully explained and documented in my letter, were still around. I formally made it clear that I wished to leave the post without first serving the mandatory two years.

Within a very few days I was invited to make an appointment with the Deputy Chief Probation Officer at Probation Headquarters – the boss of the boss of my boss – elevated levels indeed! I telephoned headquarters in Birmingham, and to my surprise, when I spoke to his secretary, was offered an appointment a very few days later – I had been expecting to wait for weeks or months. I well remember that meeting with him. Have you ever started to lean your weight against a heavy door to open it, when, coincidentally, it is opened by someone on the other side? The lack of the expected resistance can throw one quite off balance. I do not know whether he had seen my letter to the hostel Manager, but since the information about the situation must have come to him via the Assistant Chief to whom she had given the letter, I guess he probably had seen it. Anyway, I found him surprisingly prepared, and even eager, to accommodate my needs, and he invited me to apply for any advertised probation officer post I chose.

In retrospect, my experience of working at that hostel has been a great benefit to me, and to others. The experience of working under a manager of limited skill and apparently unlimited inconsistency, and the consequent effect on my own mental health has been a huge advantage to me in subsequent work, counselling staff of large organisations referred to me through Employee Assistance Programmes, both to help those trying to function under such management, and to enable managers referred to me to examine their own management styles, and changes they might choose to make.

Another benefit also resulted. Some time after I left the hostel, I heard through the grapevine that my predecessor there had returned to work, to a different Probation Officer post in the Service. I also heard that she had been unable to function, and had been allowed to retire early, on health grounds. I never actually met her, though we had several telephone conversations, but several who had known her well kept in contact with her, and later I heard that she was taking the West Midlands Probation Service to court, suing them for causing her illness. As you may know, an employer has a statutory obligation to provide a safe working environment for employees, and she was saying that the working environment of the hostel failed to fulfil this requirement, in that it had caused her to become seriously ill.

After some thought, I decided that, since my letter had been given to the Assistant Chief Probation Officer already, and probably to his boss the Deputy Chief too, it was no longer in any sense a private communication. I contacted my predecessor, and subsequently her solicitors, offering to share the letter with them. The solicitors were keen to meet with me, and were delighted with the document, particularly as I made it clear that I was very prepared to appear as a witness at any court hearing. Days before the hearing at which I was to attend as a witness, I heard from the solicitors that the case had been settled out of court, and that their client had been paid a considerable sum of money. In my opinion, the damages she received were entirely justified.

Some years later I benefited again from that experience, when a large company asked me to devise a training course to deliver to their supervisors and first line managers, to teach them to recognise stress in their employees, and to manage them in ways that would minimise this. The reader can imagine the enthusiasm with which I approached this task! The material, and especially the handouts from that course have often been of great use since then.

A few weeks after my meeting with the Deputy Chief Probation Officer, a post as a field Probation Officer at Chelmsley Wood was advertised internally, and I applied for it. I was invited for interview with the Assistant Chief Probation Officer for the area. At least, I thought it was to be an interview for the post. When our conversation started, it was immediately made very clear that the post was mine if I chose to accept it. Almost exactly a year after starting work at the hostel I left again, and began work at Chelmsley Wood.

Chelmsley Wood is an enormous housing estate, built in the middle of a countryside area by the local housing authority. Originally, it had been seen as an extremely desirable area to move to – a new estate, with countryside areas nearby and a newly built shopping centre. Those who had known the area for a long time told me that in those days a move from a Birmingham council estate to a house in Chelmsley Wood was seen as a sort of reward given to those who had been good council tenants for many years.

I had heard through the probation grapevine that Chelmsley Wood was now an area of high crime, and that working as a Probation Officer there was likely to be hard work. One colleague told me with a grin that it was the West Midlands answer to Beirut. While this was a bit of an exaggeration, my first few weeks at Chelmsley Wood Probation Officer gave me amply proof of the difficulties. One client who had offended certain (unnamed) local residents showed me the results – spectacular pictures of his car, parked outside the house where he lived with his mother and his brothers.

The photographs, taken in the middle of the night, were of his car, engulfed in flames, as a result of some anonymous arsonist. Another man, believed by certain others to be a 'grass', or police informant, returned to his flat one day to find that it had been badly damaged: petrol had been poured through the letterbox, and it had then been set on fire. In Chelmsley Wood, unemployment and poverty seemed the norm, and heroin addiction was commonplace.

The Chelmsley Wood Probation Office was a building that had originally been the local Post Office. It looked like an oversized Portacabin, and despite regular painting of affected areas, I do not think I ever saw the building entirely free of graffiti for more than a few days at a time.

Despite all this, it was a great pleasure to return to working as a field Probation Officer. Those working there were warmly welcoming, and the team seemed entirely composed of people who genuinely wanted to relieve human misery, and to make a real difference to the lives of clients and their families. I felt sure that my time at Chelmsley Wood was going to be a long and happy one. It certainly was.

I have said little in recent chapters about spiritual things, because very little changed. I had occasionally been asked to preach at St Thomas' Church when the regular preachers were not available, and for a short time Maggie and I had been leaders of a house group. Apart from that, we were just ordinary members of the Church, and of several house groups within it, over the years: house groups were reorganised with new members at intervals, so that, over the years, we got to know well many members of the Church. Sometimes, Maggie and I would sit together in the evenings, talking about the wonderful life that God was providing. Sometimes we wondered why, since we were nothing out of the ordinary as Christians, God seemed to have singled us out for special blessing. Our sons were growing up healthy and well balanced; our relationship with each other was deeply satisfying to both of us; we had a comfortable house, and a mortgage and other outgoings we could afford; we both had work that we found fulfilling and satisfying. Both of us felt sure that, once the children were older, God had more for us to do. Meanwhile, we were more than content simply to enjoy the life He was providing.

One evening in 1995, we had been chatting happily at the end of a day. I do not remember whether we had been praying, or just talking about the way that God was continuing to work quietly in our lives. I heard God speaking. Not a literal voice, you understand, just a sense of quiet certainty that the thought that suddenly appeared fully formed in my mind was from God. I silently considered the thought for a moment before sharing it with Maggie. God was saying to us, **"There will be seven years of fat, then seven years of lean".**

We discussed together what this might mean. In Old Testament thinking, seven was the number of perfection or completion. I had no idea whether this was to be a literal seven years, or whether the meaning was 'when the years are completed', or in other words 'at the right time'. Of course, this was reminiscent of the warning that God had given to Pharaoh, the ruler of the Egyptians, through Joseph, many centuries before Jesus was born. (See the Old Testament book of Genesis, Chapter 41). In the account of this in the Bible, Joseph had advised Pharaoh to build vast storehouses to store the grain from the plentiful harvests of the years of fat, so that it might be available to feed the population during the seven years of lean that would follow it. Certainly, the message seemed to be that we should be storing or saving some of our earnings over the next few years, because our earning ability was not going to go on indefinitely. I must say that I thought at the time that 'seven years of fat' meant *another* seven years of fat, because we considered ourselves already well blessed by God. The prosperity that was about to arrive was a surprise to us both.

Chapter 11

The Practice

After I left West Bromwich Probation Office, I kept in touch for some time with Nigel, whom I had met when he was manager of the addictions clinic there. While I was still at the Probation Hostel, he told me about a company for whom he had begun to work from time to time, on a self employed basis. The company supplied to large companies and organisations a programme (called an Employee Assistance Programme or EAP) to provide employees with professional counselling as and when they needed it. He explained to me that all employees of a client company had access to a 24-hour freephone number, staffed by trained telephone counsellors. If the employee and the telephone counsellor decided it was appropriate, the employee could be referred to a counsellor in the area in which they lived, for face-to-face counselling. The company was recruiting further counsellors to add to their existing countrywide network of counsellors, to work for them as and when referrals were available.

I was very interested, and contacted the company soon after. A few weeks later I sent a completed application and the company took up references I provided. Then, by appointment, a manager from the company visited me at home. Gilroy was a tall, immaculately dressed African-Caribbean man of around forty, who spoke with a refined, Oxbridge accent and moved with easy grace and confidence as I showed him to the consulting room. During the interview that followed I was impressed by the warm and friendly way in which he put me at ease, and by the very professional way in which, in a casual and informal manner, he began asking probing and insightful questions that I feel sure would quickly have revealed any major shortfalls in my counselling ability.

Despite my awareness that I was being thoroughly and expertly interviewed and assessed, Gilroy's manner somehow made me feel entirely at ease throughout the process. Of course, by interviewing me at my home, he was also creating for himself the opportunity to see the room and the building in which I would be seeing clients referred to me, and to check many other details, like the degree of security with which client records would be kept. After around an hour, he seemed to be satisfied, and began discussing the procedures that the company and its 'clinical affiliates' followed when working with clients.

Soon after, clients began to be referred to me by the company. At first, there were only a few, then, as the company got to know my work, steadily more referrals. Instead of working with just one or two clients at a time, I was now frequently working with two or three times as many, and I would look forward to returning from work to check the telephone answering machine for new referrals from the company, before preparing to greet my first client of the evening. Until this time, the number of private clients had been very small, because advertising had been restricted to occasional small and inexpensive ads in the local paper. My two sons were now eleven and fourteen years old, and I took very seriously my responsibility as the main provider to the family. Up till now, the practice had not shown any financial profit, and I really could not justify spending very much of my salary, which I regarded as the family's money, on an activity which, so far, had been at the level of a hobby or part time activity, the income from which had only partially covered the costs of doing the work. As I completed the work with each client referred to me by the company, I was required to invoice them. As, month-by-month, the EAP Company paid me for the work I had done, I paid this into a separate bank account. With a growing family, we had never been able to save very much despite the fact that we were both working and earning, and at that time our savings amounted to a few hundred pounds. I watched with some excitement as the 'hobby account' grew month by month.

I had discussed advertising from time to time with several fairly successful therapists I knew. All of these advertised in a variety of media. However, all of them had said, in response to my question, that the vast majority of those contacting them seeking therapy were responding to one advertisement in particular – the one in Yellow Pages. Two considerations had prevented me from ever advertising in Yellow Pages. The first was the very high cost.

There was a second reason. When I had been considering training as a hypnotherapist, I had phoned a number of established therapists to find out more. I had been surprised to find that, almost without exception, their phones had been answered by an answering machine, and a recorded voice invited me to leave a message after the tone. My other reason for not even considering expensive Yellow Pages advertising to elicit far more enquiries was that I had no one to answer the phone.

Maggie was often at work and our sons were at school. Even if my sons had been available, it hardly inspires confidence in a distressed enquirer if his or her telephone call to a therapy practice is answered by an adolescent. I also knew that when I had telephoned anyone in the past, I had found a little off-putting the unexpected sound of a recording, and the unexpected need to leave a recorded message, and I had always felt that this would be even more discouraging to a person in emotional turmoil, seeking help. There seemed little point in eliciting a large number of enquiries until I had some way to ensure that I did not lose a large proportion of potential clients before even speaking to them.

At this point, the solution to this problem was provided by James Middleton. When I visited him one evening, he showed me his latest acquisition, a personal pager. He explained that this was provided by a company that also provided a personalised answering service. He had been allocated a personal number to which his practice number could be diverted, and anyone who phoned would be answered by professional staff, who would answer the phone according to the script he provided, as though they were his reception staff. They would take a message, which would be paged to him. I enthusiastically asked for more details. Here at last was the final missing piece in the jigsaw! 'Coincidentally' this happened at just the time when the balance in the hobby account had grown to a size that would enable me to pay for a Yellow Pages advertisement, without using any of the earnings from my main occupation.

Another 'coincidence' happened at that time too. An NLP trainer, who had agreed to teach an introductory seminar to a group of Education Authority employees, contacted me because of a sudden inability to fulfil that commitment. I agreed to teach the seminar, aware that the level of training I had acquired meant that the task would need little preparation. One enthusiastic attendee at that seminar was a professional graphic artist, and during a conversation during a coffee break she had mentioned that she also did freelance work. For a moderate fee, she listened to my ideas about the sort of advert I envisaged, turned them into a professional looking advert, and produced for me an original of the quality required by Yellow Pages. I was surprised and delighted by the work she had done, turning my ideas for the advert into reality, and producing an ad very different from any others in the directory. I contacted Yellow Pages, and a few days later, a sales rep was sitting in my home, taking my order.

There was a wait of a couple of months before the next edition of Yellow Pages was to be printed and distributed. I was a little worried during that time: the adverts had cost me just over eight hundred pounds! What if nobody phoned? When I visited James Middleton, he reassured me as well as he could. Yellow pages advertising was effective, he told me, and I would definitely get some responses. Finally, the new edition of Yellow pages arrived on my front doorstep. For the first time, in April 1996, the new editions of the Yellow Pages for Wolverhampton and for Birmingham North included, under the 'Hypnotherapists' section, an advert for my practice. I am sad that I no longer have a copy of that original advertisement, and have long since lost touch with the graphic artist who produced it for me. A design I have used since for my cards is almost identical to that advert, and is shown below.

Within weeks, client numbers had doubled. Then they doubled again. Then numbers began to increase some more. Most days, I would finish work at the Probation Service, then drive home and prepare for three client appointments, finishing at 10.30 pm. I was also doing a full day's work on Saturday seeing clients at home. This might seem like a punishing schedule, but both the probation work and the private practice I found so rewarding and fulfilling that I would wake on a Monday morning eager and excited by the prospect of another week ahead. By 1997, the practice had grown sufficiently that I needed to reduce my probation hours, and the Service agreed to my request to become part time, reducing my working week to 30 hours. As the practice became busier, we avoided increasing our spending, and as a result, within a few years had paid off most of our mortgage, and all our other credit, like the loan we had taken out to buy a car, and another for double-glazing. As the practice increased, I progressively reduced the hours I worked each week for the Probation Service.

After much prayer, I decided to do another NLP Master Practitioner training. This time I trained with Centre NLP, a training organisation based in Leicester. As I completed the various modules of the course, I was somewhat vigilant: I did not want to experience again the ill effects of my first Master Practitioner training. I need not have worried. Jo Cooper and Peter Seal, the partners in business and in life who ran the course were very kind, very competent, and very careful to monitor the progress and well-being of their students. Studying with them was hard work, but invariably stimulating and challenging, and ultimately successful, and after successfully completing the course, I finally had my NLP Master Practitioner Certificate.

At last I could apply for accreditation as an NLP Psychotherapist. The requirements for this were very demanding, both in terms of the number of NLP training hours required (considerably more than for Master Practitioner certification) and in terms of other study. Happily, when I added up all the hours of NLP training I had done, including two separate Master Practitioner courses, I had achieved the total hours required. In addition, training was required in a variety of subjects, including human growth and development, human sexuality, and several other aspects of psychology and other subjects, all of which I had completed while training as a social worker at Coventry. The University were happy to confirm the details of this in a letter to me, thus providing the required documentary proof. The application itself was also pretty demanding, and when typed was over forty pages long. Still, finally it was done, and I posted off the ten copies that were required.

Then came the hardest part. I was invited to London, for interview, at Regents College. The interview was by a panel of four very experienced and capable NLP Psychotherapists, members of the Accreditation panel. All four were remarkably observant; they had obviously gone through my application very carefully. One had even found an error in my calculation of client numbers, which made me even more nervous. The interview lasted an hour according to my watch, but it felt like two or three hours at least. At the end of it, those four people knew more about my practice of psychotherapy than I would have thought possible, and I felt as though I had just fought ten rounds with a heavyweight boxer. As I drove home, reflecting on the experience, I knew that, whether or not I was accredited, I had put everything I could into that interview. Around a week later, I received the letter telling me that I was now an Accredited NLP therapist, and that accordingly I would be registered with the UK Council for Psychotherapy. At last, I had arrived.

Many and varied have been the people who have become clients, responding to the Yellow Pages advertising, and over the years a growing number have contacted me because others who have been clients have encouraged them to do so. In the cases that follow, names and some personal details have been changed to ensure confidentiality.

Mark was a man in his early twenties, who consulted me because of his very low self-confidence. Apart from a few weeks in a temporary job, he had been unemployed since leaving school. When we met for the first time, his lack of self-confidence was clear: he was quite unable to meet my eyes for more than a fraction of a second, and he spoke timidly and very quietly indeed, often with a slight stammer. He was very committed to working to change this, and despite the fact that he had only state benefits to live on, was entirely prepared to pay my fees in order to achieve the changes he was seeking. So extreme was his difficulty that he was quite unable to attend interviews for employment. On several occasions in the past he had been given an appointment for interview, and had managed to arrive at the door of the office where the interview was to take place, only to be overcome with fear. On each of those occasions instead of walking through the door he had turned and fled, and each time his despair and shame increased.

Exceptionally, I insisted on reducing the fees I charged him after the first few weeks, because I did not want his commitment to be blunted by financial difficulty. It was difficult and painstaking work – for him as well as for me – using hypnosis and other psychotherapeutic methods to begin to dismantle the structure of past experiences and beliefs about himself which had created and were now maintaining his lack of confidence. We also spent some time developing his social skills, and in particular his interview skills.

I remember well the day when, after some months of working with him, I received a paged message from him asking me to phone. I phoned back, asking how I could help. "Dave," he said, "I thought I'd phone you to let you know that you're due for a pay rise." Puzzled, I asked him what he meant. With glee and elation, he shouted down the phone, "*DAVE! I'VE DONE IT! I'VE GOT A JOB!!!*"

Mark continued to attend sessions with me for a while after that, but most of the work was already done. As he settled into life as an employed man, his confidence increased in leaps and bounds. Finally, we both felt that there was no need for further work, and he left the practice for the last time, extolling the work in glowing terms, thanking me profusely, and shaking my hand so enthusiastically I wondered if he was trying to detach it from the wrist.

Rose had a phobia for spiders – arachnophobia. This is a fairly commonplace problem, but Rose had the worst case of arachnophobia I have ever seen, before or since. The mere thought of a small dead spider that might be in the far corner of the room was enough for Rose to become visibly fearful. She was a young married woman and her husband worked permanent night shifts. Summer, for her and her husband, was a terrible and difficult time, and she lived indoors as much as possible, in permanent dread of encountering a spider. Before her husband went to work, he would have to search the house from top to bottom, with special attention to the floor under the bed, and to the cupboards in the bedroom, and then close and lock all doors and windows. When he left for work, she would then go to bed, even though it was still light outside, just in case he had missed a spider somewhere.

Slowly, over many weeks, Rose and I worked together to reduce the severe anxiety state from which she was suffering. Then, using NLP patterns, we spent a session working with a terrifying childhood experience involving a spider, completing a process called detraumatisation. At the end of that session, Rose was able to imagine spiders as vividly as she chose, and was apparently unable to reproduce the fear, even when challenged to do so. Still, she was not yet convinced that the phobia was gone for good. It was clear that she was going to need more proof before she could be sure, and I invited her deliberately to test out the work in the time till our next appointment.

At the next appointment, Rose told me that she had deliberately sought out spiders to test the work thoroughly, and to expose herself to their presence on a number of occasions, without ill effects. Finally, her husband had returned from work one day to find her digging in the earth under the shed. Somewhat puzzled, he asked her what she was doing, and she explained that she wanted to test out the work one last time, but try as she might, she could not find a spider anywhere in the garden! Remembering that there had been a number of large ones under the shed some weeks before, she had decided to try to find one. She told me that her husband and she were both helplessly giggling for several minutes at the absurdity of her actions before concluding, correctly, that the phobia was definitely gone!

Samuel was the owner of a prosperous medium sized business. He was in his late forties, and had a beautiful home, a car considerably nicer than I will ever own, and a devoted wife: it was his wife who had originally contacted me. The couple went abroad several times each year for lengthy holidays, and, while I did not ever ask the question, I did not envisage them travelling economy class. Despite this apparently idyllic lifestyle, Samuel was not a happy man. Under a façade of stillness and strength he had battled for many years with extreme anxiety and stress, a problem that I was later to realise is often endemic among the successful self-employed. The problem had grown steadily worse, and by the time his wife contacted me he had for many months been waking several times each night in a blind panic, realising only after some minutes awake that the nightmare he had been suffering had not been real. Symptoms would magically disappear whenever the couple went away on holiday, reappearing unabated when he returned to work.

Over the course of many weekly appointments, Samuel's nightmares became less frequent, and finally ceased. However, running his company was a source of considerable stress, and week after week he would return showing all the symptoms of stress that had preceded the beginning of the nightmares in the first place. Usually, work with a client will go on to address the causes of such stress. However, Samuel was adamant: he was not prepared to do this. Moreover, although week after week he would assure me that he would make the time to do the simple 'homework' tasks that would reduce his need to keep attending weekly appointments, he would return each week as stressed as ever, saying that he had been far too busy to complete the simple tasks that we had agreed. A few times, we tried experimentally reducing his appointments to fortnightly, and symptoms would return. Samuel was unconcerned about the idea of continuing weekly appointments: on one occasion, he told me that he regarded them in the same light as he regarded the regular visits to his home of the lady he paid to do the cleaning. I was a sort of a psychological charlady.

Samuel continued coming to weekly appointments for several years. Each week he would arrive stressed and anxious, and would leave an hour later calm and serene. Each week, I knew he wouldn't implement the simple changes and techniques that would have reduced his need to return. He finally stopped coming to appointments when he sold his business and retired, in early middle age. I understand that he is now living somewhere with blue seas, white sand, warm weather and swaying palm trees...

One lady, who had been married for several years, consulted me because of certain stress symptoms, and over the course of several months was able to completely eliminate those problems. At the session in which she told me, with some sense of real achievement, that she had been entirely problem free for many weeks, she also told me that, to her delight and that of her husband, she had become pregnant for the first time. "So what do you do for pain in childbirth?" she said, "Because I have already decided that this child is going to be born entirely naturally!"

We had around six months before the baby was due, and she had already developed good skills in guided self-hypnosis, so I expressed guarded confidence that we could work together successfully on this new issue. During the months that followed, we worked together to establish appropriate pain-blocking skills. Finally, the baby was born. The lady tells me that, at her insistence, the baby was born at home, and that the midwife and the student midwife who attended her there were amazed to witness childbirth entirely without anaesthetics, and entirely pain free.

(I should mention in passing that hypnotic pain blocking is often so effective that I am never prepared to work in this way unless a medical practitioner has confirmed that it is safe to do this. To do otherwise would be not only foolhardy but also potentially dangerous, and might mask important symptoms of disease: pain is usually a **friend**, giving important information about something that is wrong.)

One day, a paged message asked me to phone someone enquiring about therapy. I returned the call, and the woman I spoke to said that she was looking for a therapist to work with her suicidal husband. I asked for more details. The woman expressed surprise, saying that she had phoned four therapists already, and that all four had suddenly been too busy to see her husband for many weeks, once she had said the word 'suicidal'.

The caller had already discussed psychotherapy and hypnotherapy with their GP, and he had given the idea his blessing. Her husband John, she told me, had been suffering from depression for many years, and had been prescribed antidepressant medication by the General Practitioner for the last two years. He was still deeply depressed, and both he and she were beginning to despair of ever finding any solution.

When I met for the first time with John for a consultation a few days later, his wife accompanied him. It was clear that he was, indeed, very unwell. He spoke in a monotonous, melancholic voice, and moved in a slow, melancholic manner. He was preoccupied with depressive thoughts, and told me frankly that he saw little point in anything – including continuing to live. His wife, sitting in the corner of the room, interjected, "He's like this all the time!"

From the beginning, John conscientiously completed the 'homework' tasks we agreed, and over many months of work, his depression symptoms reduced in severity and frequency. Finally, for many weeks, he seemed to be entirely free of the problem. At my suggestion, he made an appointment with his doctor, who told him to halve the dose of antidepressant for a couple of weeks, and to then cease the medication altogether. Within a few weeks, the symptoms had returned, and the old depressed John was once again sitting in my consulting room. He agreed readily to my strong suggestion that he return to his doctor to discuss this. His doctor reinstated the medication, and after confirming with John that he was still seeing me, suggested that John should wean himself off the antidepressant more slowly, saying that he would leave it to John and me to decide how long this should take.

It took many months to complete this. With each slight reduction in dose, John would experience a re-emergence of depression symptoms. Only once further work had eliminated those was John ready for a further very small reduction of dose. Finally, he was free of medication and of depression. I do not think he quite believed that his freedom was permanent, and he chose to continue to book appointments with me for some months. Finally, he knew that there was no longer any problem, and that he was permanently better, and he left after his final appointment with me, walking down the road with a spring in his step.

In the year 2000, a young man called Paul became a client. He was extremely skilled in working with computers, and many months after we met he offered to build a website for the practice. Since then, many of those who have made contact seeking hypnotherapy and psychotherapy have found me through that website. The website can be found at: **www.helpishere.co.uk**. The website included a guest book where visitors to the site could leave their name and make comments, and Paul decided he would be the first to make an entry in it.

After some months of work, the problems Paul had brought to therapy were largely resolved. Meanwhile, he had become increasingly curious about the small cross that I wear as a tiepin. More and more of our weekly meetings were spent answering Paul's very probing questions about my own relationship with Jesus, and about what it meant to me to be a Christian. I have always maintained the view that, as a secular therapist, I have no more right to impose my faith on others than, say, a Christian doctor or accountant. So at the beginning I answered Paul's questions fairly briefly. Paul, however, made it clear that he was choosing to use his sessions in this way, and that this was his time, for which he was paying. His questions became increasingly searching. These sessions I found highly challenging: he was an intelligent man, and I began to look forward to my weekly 'cross examination' about my relationship with God, and about many details of the life of a disciple of Christ.

Finally, Paul decided to become a Christian. It was clear that he had his own deepening relationship with the supernatural living Jesus Christ, and had made his own decision. He lived in an area called Darlaston, some miles away from the practice, and he asked if I could suggest a Church in the area. I really had no idea. Darlaston had always been for me just a place to drive past on my way to somewhere else. I asked the minister at St Thomas', the Church where Maggie and I were members, and he gave me two or three suggestions, which I passed on to Paul. After visiting those Churches, Paul visited several others, before finally becoming a member of St. Lawrence's Church, in the Centre of Darlaston. Paul continued his weekly visits to me, and I began hearing more, week by week, about his new Church. Paul got to know the minister and his wife and other church members very well over the months that followed.

Chapter 12

St Lawrence's Church

At one appointment, the client Paul passed on to me a message from the minister of his Church: he was fascinated by what Paul had told him about the Christian hypnotherapist through whom he had found out about Jesus, and he suggested that we might meet.

Some weeks later, I met for the first time with the Rev. Dave Wills, at his rectory in Darlaston. Somehow, he seemed a little unlikely as a vicar: a little younger than me, short, plump and balding, he spoke in a straightforward, direct way, with a strong cockney accent. Although we were very different from each other in some ways, we clicked immediately, and spent some hours sharing together about the ways in which God had worked in our lives. For me the time passed as though it was a few minutes. As I chatted with Dave, I also felt a growing conviction that our meeting was more than chance. I knew that there was already one Reader at St Lawrence's, and Dave knew that I had trained as a Reader. I found myself saying, "Dave, this might be completely off the wall, but I wonder whether St Lawrence's could use another Reader? Dave was thoughtful for a moment, and then he said that he did not think that the idea was off the wall at all, and suggested that over the days ahead we should pray about it, and see what happened.

It was some weeks later after much prayer that I went to a service at St Lawrence's Church for the first time. I slipped into the Church quietly, a few minutes before the service was to start. I had already seen the Church building, because Dave had given me a brief guided tour when I visited him. It was a very traditional Victorian building, and I was not surprised to find that the service I had come to was traditional too. This was very different from the very modern and informal services at St Thomas'. So I was more than a little surprised to find that, in the very ordinary and rather formal Church of England service in the archaic language of the old 1662 Prayer Book, I experienced the strongest sense of the presence of God that I had experienced for many years. The experience was strong enough that I knew that I should go there again.

Often, when we revisit the scene of a strong and positive experience, it can be something of a disappointment – but not in this case. The welcome with which this newcomer was greeted was remarkable, and each time I went to a service there, the conviction grew that God was calling me to minister there as Reader.

Maggie was a little reluctant about the place to start with. She came with me sometimes to services at St Lawrence's, but continued to be a member at St. Thomas' Church for many months, and to attend services there too. Then one evening Maggie was at a meeting at St. Thomas' Church. Those at the meeting were invited to spend a few moments in prayer, and Maggie began silently asking God if there was more He was asking her to do. For some time, Maggie had been doing some visiting to the bereaved on behalf of the Church, and wondered if there were others she should be visiting. Telling me about it later Maggie could scarcely suppress her excitement. The answer had come loud and clear in her mind: **"St Lawrence's'"**. Maggie was excited and pleased to have her own calling from God to St. Lawrence's, independent of me – her own confirmation that St Lawrence's was the Church where God intended us to be.

Over the months that followed, we slowly got to know the members of our new Church. After some months, I was invited to preach at services several times. Then Dave Wills told me that at the next meeting of the PCC (short for Parochial Church Council) the proposal that I be invited to be licensed as Reader at St Lawrence's was going to be discussed. Several members of the Church asked me if I was nervous. I had to say that I wasn't. I felt very strongly that this was all God's doing, and that was why I was there. I had learned from past mistakes, and I knew that I only wanted to be licensed as a Reader at the Church if the calling was from God – and it was somehow very easy to surrender to Him the outcome of that meeting.

The following day, I heard by telephone from Dave Wills that the PCC had formally passed a motion inviting me to minister there as a Reader. Some months later, at a service at St Lawrence's Church, I was formally licensed by the clergyman responsible for local ministry in the diocese, at a special service. That was a little over six years ago, but I still remember well one particular moment in the service, when the clergyman turned to the congregation and formally asked those in the crowded Church, **"Will you support him in this ministry?"** I also recall the real enthusiasm in many voices, and the feeling of real warmth and support I experienced as they read the response from the service card: **"With the help of God, we will!"** From that day to this, they always have.

It was some months after this that we heard a less welcome piece of news. Maggie's father and mother had been members of their local church for many years, and her father Sidney, had died several years before. His funeral service had been packed with friends. Maggie's mother, Elisabeth, now elderly, had been unwell for several years with cancer, and now her illness was becoming steadily worse. The doctors were clear that there was little more that they could do to treat the disease, and that she was expected to die. Elisabeth, a woman with her own deep relationship with God, seemed very calm about this, and in her conversations often showed more concern about how others were coping with her impending departure than with her own feelings.

I well remember our last Christmas with Elisabeth. As Maggie and I and our two sons sat together with her in the lounge of Elisabeth's flat exchanging presents, each of us watched as the recipient opened each present they were given. A present was given to me, wrapped in Christmas paper, from Elisabeth. I thanked her, and began opening the present, a little surprised that, in her weakened state, she had been able to think about presents for others, and I wondered if she had sent Maggie out to the shops to buy them. Then, as I recognised the present I had been given, I was stunned for several minutes, speechless, as I realised its implications.

For years, Maggie and I had visited often with our two sons. One time, when Sidney was still alive, among the many and varied ornaments that covered every surface in their home, I had noticed a blackened old metal cup with a stem, shaped like a wine glass. Curious, I had looked at it more closely, and although it was black with tarnish, I had recognised a beautiful piece of early Victorian silver, exquisitely engraved. It had seemed to me a shame for so lovely a piece of work to be in so neglected a state, and I had asked for permission to polish it. Thereafter, a treat that I looked forward to whenever we visited was to carefully clean and polish that fine piece of Victorian craftsmanship.

Now, in the middle of the torn Christmas paper in my hand, I was looking down at the beautiful silver cup I had so often enjoyed. For a moment, I thought that maybe she had given me the cup just because she had no opportunity to buy any other presents, and it seemed wrong for me to accept this from her. Then I realised what Elisabeth had already realised, and thought about. She would soon have no further use for this, or for any other material possession. I sat for several minutes, stunned and open-mouthed as I came to terms with this new evidence that soon she would no longer be with us. Elisabeth sat silently, watching me with a half smile as she patiently waited for me to come to terms with all of this. For a moment, I remembered many years earlier, when Maggie and I had been on a cross-channel ferry, about to embark on our way to visit her sister in Germany. The large boat had been preparing to leave its moorings, and the crew were casting off, one by one, the mooring ropes that bound the boat to the quayside. Elisabeth was casting off.

As her mother became steadily weaker, Maggie took extended leave from her work, and went to stay with her mother in Chelmsford, so that she could care for her. Maggie's brother and his wife travelled from their home in Canada to visit Elisabeth for the last time. Maggie's sister travelled from the convent in Germany where she had been a nun since before Maggie and I first met, and spent time with Elisabeth.

Maggie, in one of her many very deep conversations with Elisabeth, told her what I had thought was the meaning of her Christmas gift, that she was severing her links with this world and this life. Elisabeth agreed that was exactly what she was doing. Some weeks later, I visited the flat, a few days before Elisabeth died. I was there to visit Maggie, as she was caring for her weakening mother. Maggie told me that her mother was asking to see me. Though too weakened to sit up in her bed, she smiled as I entered the room, and we talked together quietly, sharing our conviction that God was in control here. She asked me to be sure to look after her daughter, and I assured her that I would. Finally, too weakened by the effort of talking to continue any longer, Elisabeth met my eyes and said slowly, deliberately and with quiet emphasis, **"and... now... I... let... you... go."**

Soon after this, Elisabeth died. Her wish had been to die without family around her, and at her request Elisabeth was admitted to a hospice at which she had previously stayed. She died very soon after. By 'coincidence' the nurse who cared for her in those final hours was a Christian who, shortly after her conversion, had been a member of the same Church as Elisabeth and Sidney. Elisabeth had had been responsible for teaching her, on behalf of her Church, about her new faith, and the two knew each other well. Both Elisabeth, and Sidney her husband, had been members of their Church for many years, and it is a tribute to the love with which they were regarded that Elisabeth's funeral was as thronged with mourners as Sidney's funeral had been. Both were to me a source of much inspiration, and a wonderful example of humility, real gentleness and love.

In her will, Elisabeth had left everything divided between her three children, and after the flat had been sold and affairs wound up, Maggie received her inheritance. We had no immediate need for the money, having paid off most of the mortgage on our house some years before out of the private practice earnings. We were not expecting to need the money in a hurry, so we put the money into a savings account at the bank, which paid a good rate of interest, but would require 60 days notice of any withdrawal.

Shortly before we did this, Maggie asked me whether we should **tithe** on the money. I had better explain what that is. A **tithe** is a tenth. Since many centuries before Christ, the normal minimum amount the Bible says God expects His people to give away has been one tenth of their earnings. For many reading this book, this may be something you already know all about. For those who have not heard about this before, there are many references to tithing in the Bible, and perhaps the clearest is in the last book of the Old Testament, the book of Malachi, Chapter 3, starting at verse 8.

For some years, we had always tithed, or given away one tenth of our net earnings. Some of this went to the Church; some went to other Christian causes, for homeless, famine relief and other needs. I had already thought about the question Maggie asked me about tithing, without coming to any firm decision. I suggested that the inheritance was not like earnings, and that perhaps we didn't need to tithe on it. Maggie nodded and said OK, and that was the end of the conversation.

By this time, I was working only a few very part time hours as a probation officer, and most of my earnings were from the private practice – I was seeing around 20 to 25 clients each week, and I had become used to the fact that, as clients got well and no longer had the need to see me, other people would contact me to ask about therapy. ***Suddenly, that stopped happening.*** Over the next month, there were almost no new people contacting me, and the number of clients I was seeing each week fell sharply. I tried not to worry, and to trust that God had everything in hand. Then at the end of a week I looked at my diary and saw that I had only 8 client appointments booked for the week following. I was finally (some might say very belatedly) ready to fall on my knees in prayer.

Feeling somewhat desperate, I asked God what on earth was happening, and why the practice suddenly seemed to be failing. The answer came very quickly and very clearly in my mind. **"You have thousands of pounds on which you haven't paid the tithe. *How can I honour disobedience?*"**

Maggie was at work as I prayed, and when she came home, we sat down with a coffee to chat, and I said that maybe we should tithe on her inheritance after all. Maggie looked slightly alarmed. "Hang on a minute! Why the sudden change of heart?" As I told her about the prayer time, unbeknown to me, she briefly prayed as she listened to me, saying to God that, if this was really from Him, He could give her specific guidance about what the money was to be used for, so that it was not just giving for the sake of it.

Maggie suddenly asked me to wait a moment, and from among a pile of papers picked up a newsletter from friends of ours, a missionary couple working in Bulgaria. She looked at the newsletter for a moment, then without a word went to the phone in the hall. I waited for a moment, then decided I should follow. As I walked into the hall, I heard Maggie speaking into the phone: "Hi Brian! In the newsletter you mentioned the desperate need for an ambulance in Sliven. (A town in Bulgaria.) How much would that cost?" She paused, and I heard the tinny sound of Brian's voice through the earpiece of the phone. "Brian, are you sitting down?" said Maggie, "Because that's the amount we have to give you." I heard the yell of surprise and delight from Brian!

Everything was settled. The next day, I would go to the bank, and give 60 days' notice on one tenth of the money Maggie had inherited. Then, 60 days later, we could withdraw the money and pay the tithe. Maybe then business would improve. On my way back from the bank, the pager on my belt started silently vibrating. Glancing briefly at it to read the message, I realised that it was someone enquiring about therapy, and asking for a call back. Over the next few days, the pager seemed almost alive, and I lost count of the number of people who were suddenly contacting me to discuss becoming clients. By the start of the next week, I was back to seeing around 25 clients a week.

Some comment is appropriate here. We all hear, from time to time, of Christians who are in financial need, and of Churches that are desperately short of money. At the same time, of all the teaching in the Bible, **tithing** is the one that is least often heard about, and least often referred to from the pulpit, in the sermons that are meant to be a major part of the Church's expounding of God's word to the Christians who are its members. I guess this is for two reasons: either the preacher is not personally tithing, in which case he or she does not feel able to teach about it, or the preacher is tithing personally, in which case he or she feels that to preach about it would be boastful, or 'blowing one's own trumpet'. The other reason is that when a Christian tithes, he or she often becomes more prosperous; so when he or she does speaks of tithing, those listening are inclined to think, "Well yes, it's all very well for you but..."

You may remember Dave Smith, who came to live with Maggie and me after he became a Christian. When he moved into our home, he was homeless, and his only income was the state benefit he received as unemployed. All the indications were that he would remain in that state for a long time: he was in his late fifties, and to the best of my knowledge had no qualifications. He had been told that he should expect to remain on the housing list for at least two years before there was any prospect of being offered council accommodation. *He began tithing on his state benefit*, putting one tenth of the benefit he received into the collection plate at Church each week. Within a short time, as you may remember, he was employed in well-paid work, and living in his own very pleasant council accommodation.

The Bible says very clearly in that passage in Malachi that a result of tithing is material blessing. Do we dare to entertain the thought that maybe that's true? When Maggie and I started tithing, we were not well off, or wealthy. We were a young couple with a large mortgage, and permanently tight finances. We have experienced the results for ourselves. May I earnestly encourage you, Christian, reading this, to try it for yourself? (By the way, my limited knowledge of others who have begun giving a tenth suggests that it works for non-Christians and atheists too). It may be that the lack of tithing, and the lack of teaching about tithing in our Churches is a major cause of much financial hardship.

It was, of course, a great blessing to be working in my own thriving therapy practice, with clients who really appreciated the work we were doing together. However, the blessing of all those clients had a down side too – because all of them were coming to our home. That left little time or space for ordinary life in the home, especially since the inside walls were not very soundproof, which meant that, if I was seeing a client, anyone else had to be very quiet indeed, and to avoid flushing the toilet because the cistern when it filled made a noise like a screaming banshee! The strain of this began to take its toll on both of us, but especially on Maggie. Finally, we realised that we would need to think about somewhere else to run the practice, or somewhere else to live.

Our savings had been boosted, of course, by the inheritance my wife had received from her mother, and this might be just enough to buy a very cheap house. After some looking around at properties and much earnest discussion and prayer, we concentrated our search for housing in the Darlaston area. Through our membership of the Church there we already knew a lot of people there, and housing in Darlaston was comparatively inexpensive. Finally, we found a house, which had everything we absolutely needed, though it had little beyond those bare necessities. It was a small mid-terraced Victorian house that seemed to have been modernised over the years by a succession of keen but not very skilled DIY enthusiasts. It had one big advantage – we could afford it! We were shown around the property by the couple that owned it: they were selling because they were seeking a divorce. We put in a good offer, and the estate agent told us that he expected the offer to be accepted.

Some days later, we heard from the agent again. The couple had taken the house off the market. They had decided to try again to make their marriage work.

Many weeks and much searching later, we found another very basic Victorian mid-terraced house in Darlaston that came within our very limited price range. The house was empty, because the old lady who had lived there had died. We put in an offer, which was accepted by the family members who had inherited the house. All seemed well, until we read the surveyor's report. The foundations were unstable, and the house was very slowly falling down. We withdrew our offer, giving to the owners of the house the surveyor's report, for which we had no further use.

Some days later, after much prayer and discussion, Maggie and I were soberly reviewing the situation. We had spent many months looking for a house, and twice, when we had finally found one that would do, the door had effectively been closed to us. We wondered whether God had other plans, and did not intend us to live in Darlaston, though we had both been sure that He did. Then Maggie noticed details of a house in the local paper, a semi-detached house in Darlaston that was to be sold by auction. The guide price given by the auctioneers was certainly within our budget; in fact it was below the price of either of two houses we had attempted to buy.

Those who have attempted to buy a home at the lower end of the price range will know that the search is full of disappointments, and we both wondered what was wrong with this one. Still, we got into the car, and drove to the address of the house to take a look, and subsequently we were shown around the property by the auctioneer. Comparing notes later, we found that both of us had experienced the same irrational feeling (unfamiliar to us both) that somehow the house itself was welcoming us. From the moment we saw it, we fell in love with it. Both of us hardly dared to hope that we might get such a beautiful second home.

There was a reason why it was for sale by auction. Since the present owners had bought the house, the Coal Board had found somewhere in their archives an old Victorian map of old mine workings. The maps showed a small mineshaft in the front garden, about forty feet from the house, although there was no sign of it when we looked at the place where the map showed it to be. Because of that, it was very difficult indeed for anyone to get a mortgage to buy the house, and the owners had been unable to sell it through an estate agent. This was, of course, no problem for us: thanks to Elisabeth's bequest, we had cash. According to the Coal Board, the mine had been closed in 1900. The house had been built in 1930, and in the last few years had survived two earthquakes, one of which had its centre in Dudley, only a couple of miles away from the house. That earthquake had been a severe one. At the time of the quake, I had been in our home on the other side of the town, some ten miles from Dudley, and I had felt strongly the violent shaking of the ground even at that distance.

At the auction, we were one of only two bidders for the house, and the price we paid for it was exactly the guide price the auctioneers had advertised – around half the price for which similar houses in the area had been sold. Once the solicitors had completed the sale, we got the keys, and, sitting in our new house which came complete with carpets, a cooker, and a washing machine that looked almost new, we looked at each other in some amazement, thanking our wonderful Lord for providing such a lovely house, and deeply thankful that He had closed the door on our attempts to purchase the other two Darlaston houses.

Over the months that followed, we had the great luxury of continuing to live at one house, while we decorated the new one, then the great fun of buying furniture to fill it. We had expected to use every penny of our savings just to buy a house, and that would have been the result if we had bought either of those other two houses. As it was, we had some thousands of savings to complete decorating and other small pieces of work on the house, and to furnish it to our taste, before we finally moved in. That was five years ago, in 2002. For both of us, the irrational feeling that the house itself somehow welcomes our presence remains to this day, and we have both said that we have never felt so completely at home anywhere.

Since then, we have continued in much the same way. Maggie has continued to work part time as a nurse. In 2004, the demands of the busy practice became such that I could not continue working even my part-time ten hours a week as a probation officer, and I resigned from the probation service. You may remember the prophecy about seven years of fat, and seven of lean. Well, the year 2002 was seven years after the prophecy, and as yet there is no end in sight to the prosperity that followed it.

We are still in touch with Paul. When he had no further need for a therapist, we became personal friends – not surprisingly, as we were, of course, members of the same Church. A few years ago, he met a lovely young woman through a Christian dating website, and Maggie and I were delighted when we were invited to the wedding. I felt doubly honoured when both bride and groom, having cleared the idea with the minister, made it clear that they wanted me to preach the sermon at the service! The couple now live in Scunthorpe. Paul has now gone to university as a mature student, studying for a degree in computing.

Paul was the first but not the only client, having addressed the problems that brought him into therapy, to decide to continue booking appointments to ask me about the cross that I wear and what it means to me, and a small minority of other clients have since become Christians, including a few who, like Paul, have since become personal friends. Others have chosen to continue booking appointments, using me not so much as a therapist, but more like what Roman Catholics call a 'spiritual director'. Hypnotherapy and NLPsychotherapy are powerful ways to enable a person to make the changes they desire in thinking, behaviour, feelings and other aspects of themselves: my experience is that Jesus is far more powerful still, once sincerely invited into the life of a person who understands the decision they are making to follow Him. It is a source of great joy to me to see some of these as they discover for themselves the joy of increasingly becoming the person you always wanted to become.

Still, my rule for myself had never changed: I am a secular therapist, the majority of clients do not ask about the cross on my tie or about my faith, or they ask briefly but choose not to ask further. I have no more right to impose my faith than, say, a Christian doctor, or solicitor. I still gain great satisfaction and joy from the psychotherapy work, and from feedback and comments from clients such as the small minority who have chosen to make entries in the practice website guest book. (See Appendix.)

Jesus said, "I tell you the truth"... "No one who has left home or brothers or sisters or mother or father or children or fields for me and the gospel will fail to receive a hundred times as much in this present age (homes, brothers, sisters, mothers, children and fields..."

So how do I compare what I enjoy now with what I gave up at the start of this adventure? There really is no comparison. We gave up a house that was mortgaged to the hilt, and I gave up a job and a career I hated. Now, we have two houses, one to live in and one for me to work in, and I have work that is a positive joy and blessing to me. When I came to Christ, my marriage was in great difficulty. Now, it is a deeply fulfilling source of real joy, and Maggie says that too. Our oldest son is now a doctor of physics, a researcher at the Space Research Centre at Leicester University. Our youngest son, after several years working in commerce, has just returned to university to train as a teacher. Both are fine, upstanding young men we are proud of, and both are active Christians too. We are members of a Church where we feel warmly accepted and appreciated for what we do and for who we are, and we have a wonderful circle of friends, in the Church and outside it. Every aspect of life is fruitful and positive, and I can say to God, as the psalmist says in Psalm 23:

> **"You prepare a table before me in the presence of my enemies. You anoint my head with oil. My cup overflows."** (Psalm 23: 5)

If anyone, reading this, is wondering about becoming a Christian, or disciple of Christ, I can only say that I heartily recommend it – or rather, I heartily recommend Him!

Chapter 13

Postscript – Events since the book was published – added 2013

The Prophecy Fulfilled

The preceding book was published in 2007. Nothing has been changed for this edition, apart from correcting a few spelling and grammatical errors, and updating contact details. Events since have been significant enough that adding a further short chapter seems useful, particularly to answer questions that were still unanswered at the end of the book, in 2007.

By chance, I recently met the man who was my client, "**Ross**" when I was a probation officer. (See Chapter 9) We recognised each other immediately, though both of us had aged a little. He is in full time employment, living with his partner, in his own home, **and has never committed a criminal offence again.**

The hypnotherapy client, **Paul**, (See Chapter 11) has completed his degree in Computer Science – he got a first class honours degree. He is now intending to work in the field of Computing for a few years, before returning to University to do a PhD.

Towards the end of Chapter 12, written in 2007, I said, "You may remember the prophecy about seven years of fat and seven years of lean. Well, the year 2002 was seven years after the prophecy, and as yet there is no end in sight to the prosperity that followed it."

It is worth noting that throughout the Bible, God's purpose in prophecy has never been to give people advance knowledge of what will happen in the future. The purpose of prophecy that foretells the future is, and always has been, to enable people to **recognise the significance of events** *when they are happening.*

After the book was published, life continued much as before, for Maggie and for me, until around April 2008. At that time, I noticed a reduction in the number of clients I was seeing. Not as dramatic as the last time, but still noticeable. You may remember that this had happened to me once before, when I had not tithed (i.e. given away one tenth) on the money we had inherited from Elisabeth, my wife's mother.

This time, I knew that I had tithed, and more than tithed, on all that I had earned. (I do learn from my mistakes!) Still, I knew I should take the situation to God in prayer. Within minutes of beginning to pray, I found that I had a certainty in my mind that defied rational explanation, and which I felt sure was from God: **this was the beginning of the seven years of lean foretold in the prophecy.** I felt quite certain that this small reduction in work was going to become more pronounced, and that I should sell the house that had now been my place of work for many years.

I discussed this with Maggie, who was after all, joint owner with me of that house, though it was now some years since we had lived there. We talked and prayed about the situation, and Maggie said confidently that, if God was leading me to sell the house, then we should be obedient to His direction. I could continue to work with the reduced number of clients I was expecting, in our home in Darlaston. The income generated by the sale of the house would make up for the reduced income from the practice, and would mean that I could fairly easily become semi-retired.

Knowing what we know now about the economic events that were about to happen, the wisdom of that decision to sell the house is clear. I must say that, at the time, I still thought that the 'seven years of lean' in the original prophesy referred to us alone – I certainly did not realise that a world wide economic recession was about to begin.

The house was put on the market in May 2008, and was sold, to an investor intending to rent it to tenants, in October 2008, just as the effects of the economic recession were beginning to really bite.

Since then, we continue to feel that God has blessed our life far beyond anything we desired or deserved. Maggie has now retired from nursing. I work a couple of days each week, seeing clients at our home in Darlaston, and much of the rest of the time is taken up with Christian work, as a preacher and evangelist.

I am so grateful for the fact that, by God's grace, the first edition of this book was published before anyone (including me) had any idea that the worst economic recession for many years was about to begin – that the prophecy was 'on public record' before the recession happened, because that makes it clear that the prophecy, foretelling the "years of lean" was written <u>before</u> the world-shaking economic events that followed.

The phone number that had been my practice number was given to a family in the area, and after several people, some fairly desperate, phoned them trying to contact me, the family contacted me through the Internet, and assured me that they were very happy to give my new contact details to any who phoned them. Still, I would like to avoid disturbing them any more than necessary, so my contact details are given below:

The practice website is the same as it has always been:

www.helpishere.co.uk

I still use the same answering service, so that anyone phoning can talk to a real person, not a recording machine. The practice phone number is given below:

0845 8334458

Please feel very welcome to phone, leaving a message with staff who answer, if you wish to contact me. I return most calls within two hours, and often far sooner. The phone number is also given on the practice website.

I hope you have enjoyed the book ☺

David Carpenter
May 2013.

Appendix

Website Guest Book Entries by Clients and ex-Clients

Nothing had been done to edit the following – spelling mistakes included! Names withheld as required by publisher AuthorHouse.

15.8.06

Comments: I first met David Carpenter about 2 years ago at a time in my life when life itself seemed pointless, there was no joy anymore. Why? The diagnosis was clinical stress and anxiety, which I now believe is a growing concern of life today. You may disagree? but I'm smiling as I write that question mark and the statement itself because I didn't believe either. Stress, Huh!! And yes I'm still smiling as I write this heart felt thank you!! A thank you for the simple values I've learned that are life changing and joy abounds once more. I finally wish to add that if there are any parents struggling with their child's behaviour and you're maybe at the end of your patience or endurance, I strongly recommend investing in a hour of his time because the difference it can make, well, it could just make you smile again. Regards, Sarah **City/County** Shropshire

10.2.06

Comments: I have had about six sessions with David so far. My anxiety has almost disappeared. Make an appointment now, you won't regret it. **City/Country:** Warwickshire

17.11.05

Comments: I have been seeing David on and off for years now to help control my anger and violence. without his help my marriage would be over. Thanks Dave **City/County** West Bromwich

9.11.05

Comments: I began to see David in Spring 2004 when i suffered three panic attacks in fairly quick succession. With his help, guidance and understanding i managed to overcome all my problems, so much so that later that year i got married, changed jobs, moved house and moved to another country all in around 2 months without any further panic attacks. David is an amazing man and i recommend him to anyone. Thanks David, you will never be forgotten. Andrew **City/Country:** Burton on Trent UK

7.10.05

Comments: I have now been to hypnotherapy twice with David and have been amazed by the effect it has. I was very skeptical before trying this apporach but now I believe it will reduce the level of anxiety I feel. **City/Country:** Birmingham UK

21.9.05

Comments: I started seeing David a few months ago to help with Irritable Bowel Syndrome. I was suffering from it extremely badly, I couldn't even venture out of the house without being affected. Thanks to him, my nervousness and anxiety levels are now almost at normal levels. An intelligent, friendly and compassionate man, I look forward to our sessions together. Give him a call! **City/Country:** Walsall

7.8.05

Comments: Thank you David for the help you have given me over the last three months. My anxiety levels are now at normal level which is a huge relief to me. I would recommend anyone who is thinking of Hypnotherapy to do it, with you of course! **City/Country:** Staffs

4.3.05

Comments: David Carpenter is a truly remarkable, compassionate and inspirational man. At a time when I needed help, he was there for me. David's gentle, sympathetic nature and kind, comforting words of encouragement helped me when my daily life was being controlled by anxiety and panic attacks. Do NOT suffer needlessly. Do NOT br afraid or cynical because David can help. Mere words cannot convey my grqatitude to David for his help and guidance. Life is so much better now. **City/Country:** Staffordshire

30.1.05

Comments: It has been 2 months now since David discharged me from his care.I am pleased to say that with his non-judgemental approach to my problems,he has changed my life dramatically. Where only 6 months ago I saw only problems and anxieties, I now find wonderful things happening to me in all areas of my life. Dont waste anymore time worrying..CALL HIM ! NOW ! It will probably be the single most important move you ever make in your life to put you back on the road to sanity .David instills a sense of confidence & self worth into his clients.YES!! We are all that good.! Sometimes we need another person to help us to recognise how good we are! David is that person. Call him. Its that easy.

19.12.04

Comments: I have just recently found my first job as an Airline Pilot. It's been a very long and difficult journey which culminated in my having attained the neccessary qualifications, and then, somewhat mysteriously, not being able to find a job. I experimented by seeking David's expertise, and I'm convinced that he gave me that extra bit of confidence that was neccessary for me to succeed. I would highly recommend David to anybody that finds themselves needing more self belief.

12.11.04

Comments: what can i say early this year was the lowest point of my life i can truely say if it wasnt for david i WOULD NOT BE HERE NOW, when u think all hope is is gone and things cant get anyworse out of the "madness" , like a guardian angel came help from david, today im a totally new person loving life, work, and family life. my husband and family and friends cant belive the change in me and without davids helps this new me would never have been found, thanks will never be enough but spreading the "happy" feeling and helping others is a ripple effect that is thanks all in itself if anyone you know needs help for whatever reason then dave is the man to see. **City/Country:** staffs

3.11.04

Comments: David has helped me over an extremely hard period of my life including the recovery from being sexually abused as a child and a marriage break-up. With his help I have come through and have also dealt with and overcome many phobias. Just to know that his help is there - thank you. **City/Country:** Stafford

12.10.04

Comments: I came to see Dave last year, to see if he could cure my fear of flying. after about 4 sessions, he said he had got rid of my 'fear', but I felt no different and remained sceptical, right until I got on the plane. Once take off started, which is when my fear was always the worst, the feeling in my stomach had disappeared, and has not returned since. I was amazed, and considering I went to see Dave completely sceptical that he could cure me, I am now twice as impressed than anyone else that he could do this for me. I would, and have done, recommend him to anyone with a fear like mine, I no longer dread going on holiday because of the flight!! **City/Country:** Cannock, Staffordshire

17.9.04

Comments: I've used 3 or 4 hypnotherapists in the past and David Carpenter was one of them. A genuine and caring guy and I would recommend him to anyone. **City/Country:** Lancs., UK

13.7.04

Comments: I have been a client of David's for a couple of months now, and have noticed some significant changes occurring. My confidence is improving a lot, and I'm accelerating rapidly towards my career objective of becoming an Airline Pilot. **City/Country:** Staffordshire, UK.

20.6.04

Comments: After visiting David for just a few weeks my life has changed immensely, David has helped me change my outlook on life, showing me how to believe in my self again, my anxiety levels are now very low and my confidence is growing all the time. Knowing i can visit David again when ever I want is a comforting thought. THANK YOU DAVID. **City/Country:** WALSALL/UK

9.6.04

Comments: If you need help. you came to the right place. Several weeks ago I found the courage to contact David & I am so glad I found the help I so desperately needed. Today I am a different person thanks to David's help and expertise. DONT WAIT A MOMENT LONGER..CALL HIM ! **City/Country:** Birmingham, West Midlands. U.K.

6.4.04

Comments: I would like to tell anyone out there who is suffering from depression or anxiety don't hesitate to call David Carpenter. I have just finished seeing David and i am a new women now. I can not thank him enough for his help in getting over my illness. Visiting David was much better than any prescription given by my doctor.

There should be more people like David Carpenter in the world.
City/Country: Birmingham

12.9.03
Comments: Working with David has been very helpful to me in managing stress and anxiety. **City/Country:** UK

2.6.03
Comments: The impact the therapy David has given my wife Vicky is amazing, Vicky's quality of life is improving, she has suffered with Depression for a number of years, But we can see the light at the end of the tunnel. Thanks. **City/Country:** Wolverhampton.

11.5.03
Comments: I first saw David 5 years ago with an eating disorder. We then worked on pain relief during childbirth and midwives still talk about my amazing delivery at home. He also cured me of my fear of heights. I always return to David when I start to "lose my marbles". The door is always open. And it's better than Prozac! **City/Country:** Willenhall, UK

8.2.03
Comments: Currently undergoing treatment with David and finding the therapy really helpful. Excellent service from David if anyone is considering therapy. Web site easy to read and fully explained, very user friendly. **City/Country:** West Midlands

10.10.02
Comments: Hi David Just to let you know that the last four months have been incredible. My family, colleagues at work, and most importantly myself cannot believe the change in me. I am extremely grateful for your time and patience. If anyone is thinking about seeking help do not hesitate to contact David, He's excellent! **City/Country:** West Midlands

3.4.02

Comments: Hi David, Just wanted to say thank you once again for helping me to change my life. I was very low and 2 stone over weight, due to the fact I comfort ate and couldn't break the habit. I'm now 2 stone lighter and much more confident. I will continue to recommend you to people who are so impressed by my slimmer frame. Thanks David. Regards Carol.

14.1.02

Comments: I wouldn't be where I am today if it was not for you David. THANK YOU **City/Country:** Birmingham

24.8.01

Comments: Thank you David. You have gave me new energy - I can do things I thought I would never do again because of you. I would highly recommend you to anyone. If anyone is nervous about taking this step and going to see David, I'd say go, he is definitely the best. Thank you once again. **City/Country:** Birmingham

24.7.01

Comments: Hello David, Thanks for your support. I find the therapy sessions with you extremely inspiring and helpful. I would highly recommend your input. **City/Country:** West Midlands, UK

22.5.01

Comments: You really cannot convey in a website the way that this sort of treatment can change a person's life for the better. I can recommend David highly.

11.5.01

Comments: I was a client for some time and I appreciate all the work that you have done, it has really made a difference. **City/ Country:** Darlaston, U.K.